INTRODUCTION TO
MODEL
RAILROADING

Jeff Wilson

KALMBACH BOOKS

Kalmbach Books
21027 Crossroads Circle
Waukesha, Wisconsin 53186
www.Kalmbach.com/Books

Published in 2011
15 14 13 12 11   1 2 3 4 5

Manufactured in the United States of America

ISBN: 978-0-89024-792-1

Publisher's Cataloging-In-Publication Data

Wilson, Jeff, 1964-
   Introduction to model railroading / Jeff Wilson.

   p. : ill. (chiefly col.) ; cm. -- (Model railroader books) -- (Model railroader's how-to guide)

   ISBN: 978-0-89024-792-1

   1. Railroads--Models. 2. Railroads--Models--Design and construction--Handbooks, manuals, etc. I. Title. II. Title: Model railroading III. Series: Model railroader books.

TF197 .W5456 2011
625.1/9

Contents

A Chicago, Burlington & Quincy freight train passes Portage Tower on my old HO scale layout. The layout was designed to capture the flavor of the Burlington's line along the Mississippi River in northern Illinois circa 1964. It's just one example of what can be done with a permanent layout.

Introduction

Welcome to the world of scale model railroading! It's a hobby that has many facets and one that appeals to a broad spectrum of people with interests in several diverse areas. This book provides basic information on the hobby with lots of tips on how to get started with building models, running trains, and planning and putting together a model railroad.

Scale models

This book focuses on the hobby of scale model trains, in which modelers aim to build and detail their models to represent the real thing as closely as possible. The two most popular modeling scales are HO and N. We'll concentrate on those two scales but also touch on Z, S, and O scales as well. Some modeling projects and products are scale specific, but many basic

techniques and ideas—such as scenery, track planning, benchwork, and wiring—apply regardless of scale.

We won't be covering toy trains, such as classic O gauge Lionel and Marx and S gauge American Flyer models. Although toy trains represent the real thing, they generally aren't built to scale and tend to be more caricatures than accurate models. There's nothing at all wrong with the toy train

hobby, but it doesn't match the focus of this book.

Garden railroading in G (and other large scales) is another terrific modeling option, but it is a hobby unto itself. There are a number of books and publications that can help you if that is your interest.

Also, this book focuses on North American model and prototype trains. There are many outstanding model railroads and products based on European and Asian prototypes, but space precludes providing details on them. All modeling references are likewise based on North American standards.

Multifaceted hobby

People are drawn to scale railroading for a number of reasons, and most are attracted by the modeling. Even non-hobbyists are intrigued by accurate, realistic models of buildings, trains, and scenery. The trains add the element of motion, which sets model railroading apart from other modeling hobbies such as building plastic planes and ships.

Replicating not just the trains themselves but the structures and other details that make up an entire scene is an attractive drawing point for the hobby. You can model scenes that you wish would exist in the real world or re-create a town or city as it appeared in the past.

Operations become the primary hobby focus for many model railroaders. Many individuals build model railroads specifically to operate them in the manner of a real railroad, with trains following timetable schedules and delivering cars to customers. A

small layout might have two operators each running their trains; large layouts can feature a dozen or more operators working together at once, acting as engineers, dispatchers, and yardmasters, all working together to move trains over a railroad.

Although building a basement-filling empire is the goal of many model railroaders, you don't need a huge home layout to have fun with the hobby. A small table-style layout is an ideal way to get started, and it will help you learn the many facets of model railroading. You might then find yourself ready to tackle a larger layout, but you might also discover your preference is for building and detailing models, with running trains becoming a secondary consideration. Or you may join together with other modelers, either working on a club layout or on a module of your own that can be combined with others to make a larger layout.

Some hobbies let you buy a ready-made item or two and become a full-blown hobbyist—for example, you can buy a remote-control car, charge the battery, and be ready to race. Model railroading isn't like that. Although many model railroad products are available ready to run or already assembled, building a layout does requires work on the part of the hobbyist. Benchwork must be built, track must be laid, and scenery must be crafted.

This may scare some potential modelers, but that needn't be the case. My goal is to guide you through the many facets of the hobby, providing enough information to get you started. If you get stuck, can't figure something out, or want additional information, you'll find many other books and resources available that go into greater detail on all areas of model railroading. I've listed many of these sources throughout the book.

There's no right or wrong way to enjoy the hobby. The most important piece of advice I can share is to become active: get some trains, run them, and build a couple of models. You might find yourself being drawn in a direction or interest you hadn't anticipated. Most importantly, have fun!

1

Getting started

It is important to get your trains running. A piece of plywood atop sawhorses provides a good base, and you can experiment with various track configurations. You can also add accessories and sketch potential track routes and scenic details on the plywood. This N scale GP18 is from Proto N, and the cars are from Micro-Trains.

People become involved in model railroading in different ways. Perhaps you received a train set as a gift, or you went out and bought one yourself to see what the hobby is about. Maybe you saw an operating layout or display at a train show or open house and want more information on how to accomplish the same thing yourself.

The term *armchair modeler* refers to people who stay in their chairs reading about a topic without actually tackling a project. As you read, keep in mind that the most important thing is to get started doing something: build a model, put some track on a table, and run some trains, 1.

This Atlas HO train set is an example of a high-quality starter package. It includes an oval of track, a small structure kit, a power pack, and a good locomotive with three cars.

This HO locomotive is typical of low-quality train-set offerings. Just one truck is powered, only half the wheels pick up power, and the shell is poorly detailed with an unrealistic paint scheme.

Train sets

Many people enter the hobby via a train set, **2**. Train sets can be good because they provide everything a person needs to get started: a circle or oval of track, a locomotive, a few cars, and a power pack. Some larger sets include a second locomotive; additional track with several turnouts; and perhaps some signs, telegraph poles, a small structure, or other detail items.

However, the quality of the models in a typical train set often doesn't match that of items that can be purchased separately. The quality of model railroad locomotives, cars, and accessories varies widely. And, as with other hobbies and products, you most often

get what you pay for when buying model railroad items.

The level of detail and realism is often poor in low-end, introductory train set models, **3**. You might not notice this initially, but as your experience in the hobby grows, you'll soon start to take note of things such as too-heavy (or molded-on) grab irons and other details, few (if any) separately added details, and unrealistic or inaccurate paint schemes. Components such as wheels and couplers are also often not up to par with higher-quality models.

Along with a lack of detail, train-set locomotives often have only half of their axles powered (better models have all wheels powered, with all wheels

picking up electricity). The quality of the motor and other components is also often lacking, resulting in poor performance.

4 Here's a do-it-yourself set in HO: a Proto 2000 Burlington GP20 diesel, Kadee Seaboard boxcar, InterMountain Chicago & North Western refrigerator car, Proto 2000 Alton stock car, Atlas Fuelane tank car, and Walthers Burlington caboose. The track is Atlas all-in-one.

5 This Proto 2000 F7 is typical of today's high-quality ready-to-run models. It runs smoothly, includes a DCC decoder and sound unit, has an accurate paint scheme, and features many prototype-specific details such as the plow pilot, winterization hatch on the roof, special air horn, and cutaway skirting above the fuel tank.

6 Although handy, setting up scale model trains on the floor (especially on carpet) is not the best environment for smooth operation.

You have three options when getting started. The first is to buy a less-expensive train set and gradually add models (locomotives and freight cars) to it, replacing the original items as you see fit.

The second choice is to invest more money for an intermediate- or higher-quality train set. These have fewer components at a higher price than low-quality sets, but the models are better and will continue serving you in the long term. Good options for intermediate and high-end train sets include Athearn (HO, N), Atlas Trainman line (O, HO, N), Proto 1000 (HO), S-Helper Service Showcase line (S), and Walthers Trainline (HO).

The third option is to put together your own starter set, **4**. This will cost a bit more than the other options, but you'll be able to choose exactly the models and components that you want. Let's look at putting together an HO starter set.

Designing a starter set

Start with the track. There are two basic types of track: standard, which has just the rails and ties, and all-in-one, which has plastic simulated roadbed built onto the base of the track (more details on this in Chapter 6).

All-in-one track is good for temporary setups, as it is stable and locks together securely.

You'll want enough track pieces to do some experimenting, so you can try out different arrangements on a table or floor. I'd suggest enough curved pieces to make a circle and a half in both 18" and 22" radius, a few packages of 9" straight sections, and two left- and two right-hand turnouts. Most manufacturers offer a pack of small track sections as well—these are handy for filling in odd gaps as you try various track arrangements.

This will allow you to start with a simple oval and then add the turnouts to make multiple routes, sidings, or spur tracks. You can get ideas for small layout designs by looking at published track plans or coming up with your own.

Find a locomotive that you like, **5**. You probably have an idea of what you want, perhaps influenced by trains you've seen in real life or by trains in photographs online or in books and magazines. Keep in mind that smaller locomotives (four-axle diesels instead of six-axle versions) will work better on the tight curves of sectional track.

For rolling stock, start with a caboose with a road name that matches the locomotive (a caboose is not needed if you want to model modern times—from the 1980s onward) and a few ready-to-run freight cars of various types and road names that appeal to you.

You'll need a basic DC power pack to run your train. Even if you decide to eventually opt for Digital Command Control (DCC), the power pack will come in handy as a power supply for accessories and switch machines or for testing locomotives, lights, and other electrical details on your workbench.

The chapters on locomotives (10) and rolling stock (11) provide some guidelines on selecting these items. I highly recommend browsing at a good hobby shop to get an idea of available products. People there should be able to help you if you're unsure about era, road names, and product quality or if you have other questions about getting started.

The goal of many model railroaders is to have a permanent home layout. Paul Dolkos' HO layout, which was featured in the October 2005 issue of *Model Railroader* magazine, is one such example. *Paul Dolkos*

Start running trains

Put an oval of track together, connect the power pack, put the trains on the track, and start running trains. Many people start by setting things up on the floor, **6**. This can be handy because it provides a lot of space, but although this is common for toy trains, it's not an ideal setting for scale model trains.

Carpeting doesn't provide a firm base for the track, and carpet fibers, pet hair, and dust and dirt can easily get into the gears and motor areas of locomotives and cause erratic operation. A hard floor (hardwood, tile, or concrete) is a bit better, but even if people are trying to be careful, things on the floor tend to get inadvertently stepped on—not something you want to risk with your new investment.

A table is ideal. A kitchen table might provide enough space for experimenting with N or Z scale setups but probably not with HO or larger scales. For these, a piece of plywood placed atop a pair of sawhorses makes a good temporary table. For N or Z scales, a hollow-core door atop sawhorses or a bookcase provides ample room.

Keep an eye out for detail items, structures, and other products that appeal to you. Adding them to your tabletop setup will help you picture what a future layout might look like.

Hobby shops and online retailers

You have multiple options for buying model railroad products. Although many traditional brick-and-mortar hobby shops are still going strong, others have closed or lost significant business to online retailers.

Although online sites frequently offer lower prices on many items compared to stores, don't let price be your only consideration. Shipping charges, the potential for items to be out of stock, the time it takes to receive orders, and potential problems in dealing with defective products or warranty claims can make online and mail-order purchases not worth the initial price savings.

Hobby shops offer the ability to see a product first-hand—far better than even the best photograph. Browsing through a well-stocked shop is also a great way to get ideas for your layout. Many shops offer a chance to test locomotives before purchasing, and they have display layouts or test tracks to demonstrate Digital Command Control (DCC) items and other products.

Many shops offer repair service for locomotives and other items, and they will perform setup services, such as installing DCC decoders, as well.

Hobby shops also offer a great chance to meet and talk with fellow modelers. Store personnel can also recommend local clubs that offer even more chances to meet people and learn about the hobby. Get out and visit some shops and see what they have to offer.

Online sites (especially eBay) can be great sources for finding out-of-production models or models in limited-run paint schemes. If a model has ever been produced, odds are an example of it will eventually turn up on eBay. Some of these items will have outrageous price tags, but there are also many great bargains to be found. When dealing with online auction sites or buying used items at swap meets or train shows, let the buyer beware—if you're not sure about an item, pass it by or have an experienced modeler help you check things out.

This is also a great time to try some model building. Start with a small plastic structure kit (see Chapter 8). Take your time and have fun with it, and if the urge strikes you, tackle a more-advanced plastic or wood structure kit. You can also try putting together a freight car kit as well. You'll quickly discover areas of the hobby that you enjoy.

The eventual goal for most model railroaders is to build a home layout. A layout (or model railroad) refers to a permanent setup on benchwork that combines track, scenery, trains, and structures, which differentiates it from a simple temporary setup. Moving on, Chapters 2 and 3 contain some guidelines on designing and planning a layout.

1

CHAPTER TWO

Choosing a scale and theme

Both of these are models of EMD SD9 diesel locomotives, but each dimension of the Atlas N scale model in the foreground is roughly half of the Proto 2000 HO model behind it. Choosing a scale is a matter of personal preference based on available space and available models.

One of the first decisions you need to make when getting into the hobby is choosing a modeling scale, 1. For some, this is an easy choice; for others, it proves to be a difficult decision. Some build models in multiple scales or change scales when moving or when a new inspiration hits. Let's take a look at the many factors that can influence your modeling choice.

From left to right, examples of the modeling scales are **Z**, **N**, **HO**, **S**, **O**, and **G**. *Bill Zuback*

2

Scales

You will sometimes hear the words *scale* and *gauge* used interchangeably, but there is a difference. Scale refers to the proportion between a model and the real thing. Gauge simply refers to the distance between rails of track. Thus, if you choose to model in N (1:160 proportion), you are an N scale modeler, not an N gauge modeler, but your N scale trains run on N gauge track.

Five scales compete for the attention of scale model railroaders, **2**. From smallest to largest, they are Z (1:220), N (1:160), HO (1:87), S (1:64), and O (1:48). The proportions refer to each scale's size relationship to real railcars. For example, each dimension of an HO boxcar model is 1/87 as large as that dimension on a real boxcar. The most popular modeling scales are HO and N, with the others fighting for smaller shares of the hobby.

N scale, at just over half the size of HO, was developed in the 1960s. It quickly became the second-most popular scale, with about 16 percent of modelers choosing it as their primary scale. A wide variety of products is available in N but not as much as in HO. A key appeal of N is its small size: an N scale version of an HO layout will fit in just over a quarter of the space. Or, looking at it the other way, you can pack almost four times as much layout into a given space as you could for HO, **3**.

3

Mike Danneman took advantage of N scale's small size to re-create Colorado's dramatic scenery and run long trains on broad curves on his layout, which is based on the real Denver & Rio Grande Western. *Mike Danneman*

4

5

Erik Bergstrom likes modern intermodal (container and piggyback) traffic. His HO layout, top, is based on the Burlington Northern Santa Fe in northern Illinois and includes an intermodal yard along a shelf. He has nicely captured the look of a real facility, as evidenced by the above view of a real intermodal yard—in this case, BNSF's complex in Argentine, Kans.

In the 1950s, HO grew in popularity to surpass O scale as the most popular modeling scale. More than 60 percent of modelers list HO as their scale of choice. This scale has by far the widest selection of locomotives, freight cars, structures, and other models and details. Modelers have found HO's size to be an ideal compromise between operation and detail—small enough to pack a lot of operation into a reasonable space yet still large enough for fine detailing, **4** and **5**.

The early days of scale model railroading focused on O scale, with modelers taking toy train models from Lionel and others and modifying them, and it currently is third in market share. Models in O are big, which appeals to modelers who like a high level of detail, **6**, who want a small layout focusing on switching, or who have a lot of space to devote to a model railroad. Scale product selection is less than that of HO or N scales.

S scale has also historically been dominated by toy trains (namely American Flyer), and it was the smallest practical scale size into the 1950s. Its scale is a compromise between the heft of O and the compact size of HO. As with O, several companies produce some scale equipment.

The smallest scale, Z, allows you to pack a great deal of railroad in a small space. Product choice is rather limited, and switching operations can be difficult. This isn't the scale for those who want fine detail on models, but if you just want to run trains through dramatic scenery, it's worthy of consideration.

How, then, do you decide which scale to choose? As you get to know people in the hobby, you'll have no shortage of fellow modelers who will explain to you why theirs is the "best" scale. Listen to their reasons, but don't for a minute believe that there is such a thing as one ideal scale—the right scale for someone else might not be the right scale for you.

6

Modeling in O scale allows for a high level of detail. David Stewart's Appalachian & Ohio layout is freelanced and has a 1950s-era theme based on eastern coal railroading. Here, EMD F3s lead a freight train out of a tunnel. *David Stewart*

Prototype resources

Learning about prototype (real) railroads can help you determine what you would like to do in model form. There's a wealth of information available. Books are great resources, and many railroads are represented with dozens of books covering history, locomotives, operations, and rolling stock. Many include substantial photo collections (often in color) that are invaluable to modelers. Along with specific railroads, other railroading books focus on locomotive and freight car builders and other topics.

Most major railroads that have existed from the 1900s through today have historical societies that serve as repositories of information and materials. Almost all offer regular publications, and most have websites that provide information (or links to additional information). To find websites for various societies and groups, conduct a search using the specific railroad name and the term *historical society*.

Many other websites maintained by modelers and railfans provide information such as photos (current and historical), locomotive rosters, operation descriptions, drawings and plans, and historical information. The online satellite views available through Google Earth are great for checking out rail routes, including many that have been abandoned.

Books and magazines are outstanding resources for prototype information such as photos, equipment rosters, route maps, and histories.

Nothing beats a trip to the real railroad or location you plan to model. Bring along a camera and notebook. Even if the period you plan to model is well back in the past, you'll find many details and ideas on a visit—even if the line has been abandoned.

7

Narrow gauge modeling is a popular theme. Kenneth Ehlers' Pandora & San Miguel Sn3 layout (S scale, narrow gauge, 3 feet between the rails) is based on the real three-foot gauge Rio Grande Southern that operated in Colorado into the 1940s. Here, RGS 4-6-0 No. 20 heads out of Ophir with a passenger train. *Kenneth Ehlers*

8

Paul Vassallo's Indiana Railroad is an O scale traction (electric railroad) layout. This scene depicts Mulberry Street in Muncie, Ind., circa 1940. Streetcar and interurban lines typically had tighter curves than did steam railroad rights-of-way. *Paul Dolkos*

The main factors to consider are
- the kind of modeling you are interested in
- the type of layout and operations you want to have
- the space available for your layout
- the available products in each scale that match your needs and interests

If you are interested in modeling a specific prototype railroad and/or a specific era, do some research to find out whether the appropriate models are available in each scale. A lack of available models can rule out a particular scale.

Do you have a limited amount of space but an interest in operating long trains through dramatic scenery? Then N or Z scale is probably your best choice. If you have limited space but like lots of detail and want to model city-street switching operations? Then HO, S, or O might be good choices.

Narrow gauge and electric lines

Into the early 1900s, several prototype railroads, especially in mountainous regions, were built with rails closer together than the 4'-8½" of standard gauge railroads. Three-foot gauge was the most common, with the most famous being Colorado's Rio Grande Southern and Denver & Rio Grande Western. In the east, the best known were the East Broad Top (in Pennsylvania) and East Tennessee & Western North Carolina. Two-foot gauge railroads could be found in Maine, including the Sandy River & Rangeley Lakes and others.

Models of narrow gauge equipment are indicated by an *n* after the scale, followed by the gauge of the track in feet. Thus, On3 means O scale, three-foot gauge. It's important to note that for narrow gauge models the modeling scale remains the same: all structures, details, and equipment are still 1:48. It's just that the rails are placed closer together, and the locomotives and rolling stock are built specifically to use the narrower gauge, **7**.

Another special area of modeling interest is electric railroads, **8**. These include city streetcar or trolley and interurban (inter-city) lines as well as

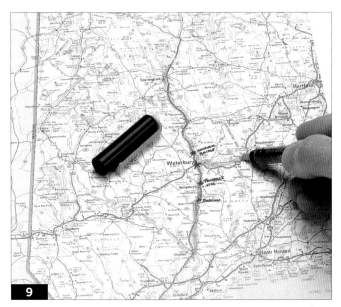

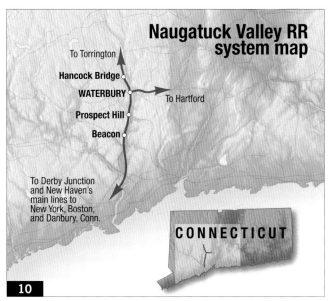

Naugatuck Valley RR system map

To Torrington

Hancock Bridge

WATERBURY — To Hartford

Prospect Hill

Beacon

To Derby Junction and New Haven's main lines to New York, Boston, and Danbury, Conn.

CONNECTICUT

Maps are handy when plotting the route of a freelanced model railroad, and using real names and routes helps make your layout theme plausible. David Popp used a highlighter to plot the route of his N scale Naugatuck Valley in western Connecticut.

heavy electric railroads. Most get their power from overhead electric wires, with a trolley shoe or pantograph atop the electric locomotive or streetcar.

Most of these ran on standard gauge track, but streetcar lines typically had tight curves and special trackwork. Interurban lines were built much like regular railroads but often with steeper grades and sharper curves. Their focus was passenger traffic, but most hauled freight as well. Heavy electric lines were standard railroads with electric locomotives.

Theme

A common temptation of beginning modelers is to acquire a hodge-podge of locomotives and freight cars merely based on what looks good. The result can be a steam locomotive running side-by-side with a modern diesel, either of which might be coupled to a train that includes a 1920s wood boxcar, a 1950s LPG tank car, and a 2000s cryogenic refrigerator car.

Nobody's telling you that you have to immediately pick a specific date to model and a specific railroad and location to re-create. Just understand that, as your experience in the hobby evolves, anachronisms will likely begin to bother you, and you'll probably want to narrow your focus for greater realism. There are a number of ways to approach a theme, including prototype modeling, freelancing, and prototype freelancing.

Prototype modeling is the idea of building your layout after a specific prototype railroad in a given period and place: a Chicago & North Western branch line in rural Minnesota circa 1950, for example. Your scenery is built to represent that specific area, with locomotives and freight cars that actually appeared on that line in the period you model. Structures and business names are selected the same way, to represent those that actually existed.

This method is popular for several reasons. First, it provides specific boundaries when selecting and building models. Modeling Norfolk Southern in 2000 means you won't be tempted by that circa-1940 New York Central passenger car or the 1930s Soo Line steam locomotive that grabbed your eye in the hobby shop. It also narrows your focus when designing towns and scenes. You're more likely to develop a realistic model scene when your pattern is one that actually existed in a specific time and place.

Also, many modelers find the history of prototype railroads fascinating. Researching the prototype can be as interesting as model railroading itself. Learning how railroad equipment evolved over time will help you model it more accurately.

Freelancing is another popular approach among modelers. This means creating your own railroad name, which

can even include lettering your locomotives and rolling stock to match the name. Towns and locations can be based on a variety of real places or simply be creations of the builder.

Freelancing means coming up with your own railroad name, town names, industries, and other details. Some modelers look at maps to find plausible routes for a railroad and select town names from along the route, **9** and **10**. Others choose names and other features based on various real-life places.

Prototype freelancing, as it sounds, is a combination of prototype modeling and freelancing. It generally involves coming up with your own name for a railroad, but placing it in a specific place in real life—often replacing a real railroad. The towns, industries, and scenes are based on actual locations. The railroad name and paint scheme are often adapted from a real railroad.

Perhaps you already know what you'd like to model. Even if you're unsure, don't be overly concerned with this and don't let it keep you from building a layout. Instead, build some models, run trains on a table, read a few books, and check out websites about real railroads, and see what interests you. Visiting a local model railroad or two can also provide inspiration.

In Chapter 3, we'll look at track planning and layout design.

1

CHAPTER THREE

Planning a layout

It's important to have a good track plan before starting construction on a layout. The track plan serves as the blueprint for a model railroad, so include as many details as possible when drawing a plan. *Jim Forbes*

You've bought some equipment, set up some track and run trains, and perhaps built a model or two. You've decided to take the next step and build a "real" model railroad, but before you start nailing track to a table, you need to develop a detailed plan for a layout, 1.

The ultimate goal of most model railroaders is to build an operating layout with track, scenery, and structures. Throughout this book, you'll see examples of scenes from various layouts that show you what is possible. Model railroads vary in size from small shelf designs a foot wide and several feet long to gigantic empires that fill entire basements or outbuildings. What you choose to build is limited by your modeling time, budget, and available space.

It can be very tempting to dive right into building a layout, especially for a beginner filled with ideas and energy. However, doing so without a clear plan can lead to a great deal of frustration when things go wrong. This approach has made many new potential model railroaders pack it in and go in search of another hobby.

If you've never built a model railroad before, start small. A small layout will let you quickly gain experience in benchwork, scenery, and tracklaying. Any mistakes you make will be on a smaller scale and easy to correct or do over.

By the time you finish a small layout, you will have a much better understanding of the time, skills, and expense needed to build a larger layout. Your modeling skills will have improved, and you will have had some time to ponder a theme, era, and prototype influence for your dream layout.

Chapter 2 discussed thinking about a prototype to model, or at least coming up with a theme and overall plan. When planning your first small layout, you don't need to know exactly what the layout will represent: it's not necessary, for example, to determine that you want to model the Union Pacific main line through Grand Island, Neb., in August 1975. It is helpful, however, to have at least a general idea of what you're trying to accomplish: perhaps capturing the flavor of eastern Texas in the 1950s. As you continue in the hobby, you'll find yourself refining your interests.

Available space

Start by determining how much room you have for a layout. Some modelers are fortunate enough to have a basement for a model railroad; others have

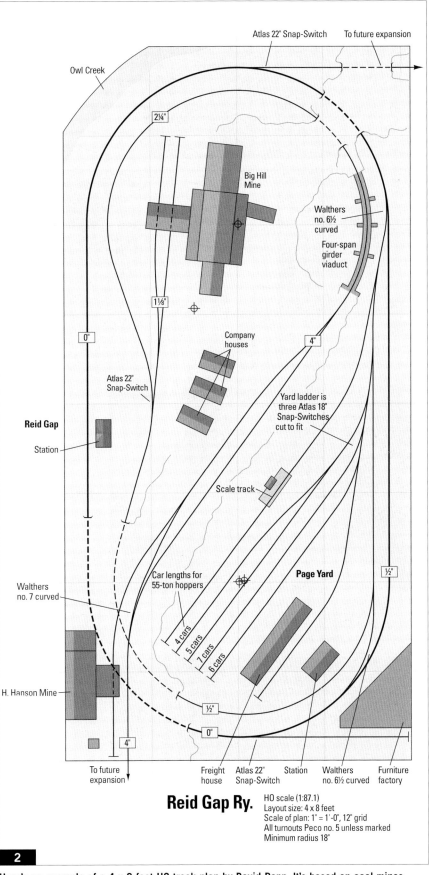

Reid Gap Ry. HO scale (1:87.1)
Layout size: 4 x 8 feet
Scale of plan: 1" = 1'-0", 12" grid
All turnouts Peco no. 5 unless marked
Minimum radius 18"

2

Here's an example of a 4 x 8-foot HO track plan by David Popp. It's based on coal mines in Appalachia served by the Virginian Railway circa 1956. Note the details on the plan regarding curve radii, turnouts, grades, structures, tunnels, roads, and bridges.

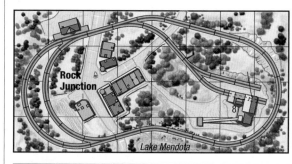

Madison Central
HO scale (1:87.1)
Layout size: 4 x 8 feet
Scale of plan: ⅜" = 1'-0", 12" grid

Rock Junction

Lake Mendota

HO scale (1:87.1)
Layout size: 4 x 12 feet
Scale of plan: ⅜" = 1'-0", 12" grid

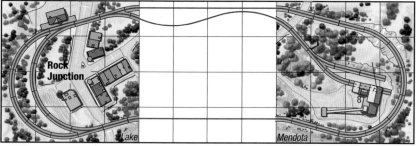

Rock Junction

Lake

Mendota

8

3

Published plans can be stretched or otherwise modified. You can cut a plan in two or more pieces and then add additional track and features between the original sections.

to find room in a spare bedroom, workshop, attic, or rec room.

Whatever space you choose, it should be a welcoming area that you enjoy being in. If it is an uncomfortable place—too hot or cold, dark, dusty, dirty or having poor lighting or headroom—you likely won't continue going there, and your layout will stagnate.

Temperature and humidity control are important—both for your comfort and for the preservation of a layout. A garage or unfinished attic might be appealing, but extremes in humidity and temperature (an attic can drop near freezing in winter or be above 100 degrees F in summer) can cause benchwork lumber and scenery materials to expand and contract, which produces kinks in track and cracks in scenery.

Basements are often touted as the ideal space for a layout, but unless

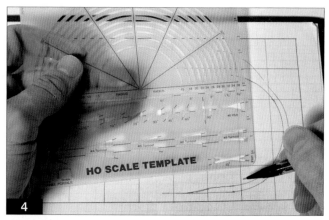

4

Tracing templates, such as this one from *Classic Toy Trains* magazine, are handy for sketching plans. Draw an outline of your table or space on graph paper to provide a guideline.

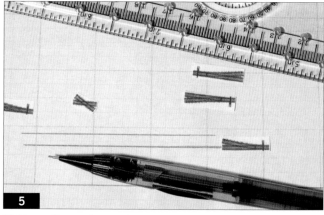

5

Walthers offers online track templates that can be printed and cut out. This helps to keep turnout dimensions realistic.

6

Laying out track components or photocopies in full size can help you visualize a scene and provide the most accurate forecast of what will actually fit in a given space.

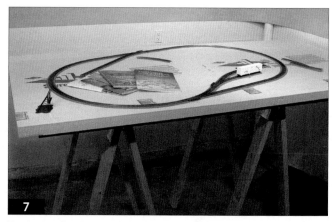

7

Track planning for table-style layouts can be done in full size. Play with various track arrangements until you find one that works.

they're at least partially finished, dust and dirt will be a constant problem. Dust and grime impede operation, causing dirty track that makes trains run erratically. Dust can also quickly build up on scenery, dulling the colors of grass and trees and leaving an unrealistic coating on structures, streets, and the trains themselves. Basements are often damp, so adding a dehumidifier will help keep humidity at a lower, constant level year-round.

A good first step is to install some type of ceiling, either drywall or drop panel grid, to eliminate much of the dust that comes down from the open joists.

Lighting is also important. A basement with only a few bulbs or fluorescent work lights won't show off your modeling in the best light. Consider adding additional light fixtures above your prospective layout area, and doing this before beginning layout construction will help you avoid headaches later.

Layout types

Layouts can be built in many different styles. Table layouts (also called island or platform layouts) are popular, especially among beginners. These generally provide room for a complete loop of track that allows for continuous running, which is high on the wish list for most people starting out in the hobby.

Because plywood comes in 4 x 8-foot sheets, many modelers adopt this size for a layout, and hundreds of track plans have been published for this footprint. The size provides enough room to have an oval (albeit a rather tight curve) plus some extra trackage in HO scale, and it allows a loop of track with broad curves in N scale.

Although a 4 x 8-foot space sounds like it would be rather compact, consider the true amount of space that such a layout takes up. The 4-foot width is too broad to comfortably reach across, so for access, you'll need to provide aisle space on at least three sides of the layout (the two long sides and one narrow side). Allowing 2 feet of space on each side (which is about the minimum although 3 feet would be better) means a 4 x 8-foot layout actually requires an 8 x 10 to 8 x 12 area. This isn't a problem in

Curve limitations

Sharp curves can limit the type of equipment you can operate. Long cars and locomotives can derail neighboring equipment. As a rough guide, only use cars 80 scale feet and longer (passenger cars, auto racks, piggyback flatcars) on broad curves. Six-axle diesels and long steam locomotives will look and run better on medium and broad curves. On sharp curves, stick with four-axle diesels, steam locomotives with eight or fewer drivers, and cars 50 scale feet long or shorter.

	Sharp	Medium	Broad
N	9¾"–11"	12"–16"	18" and up
HO	18"–22"	24"–32"	34" and up
O	36"–47"	48"–59"	60" and up

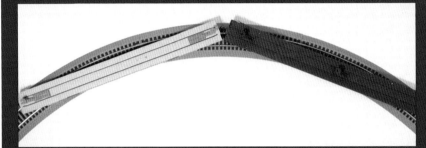

Long rolling stock doesn't look good or operate well on tight curves. These HO scale 89-foot flatcars from Walthers and Accurail likely won't stay on the track while rounding this 18"-radius curve.

On tight curves, the trucks on long equipment will turn sharply enough that the wheels hit parts of the underframe and cause a derailment.

most basements, but it approaches the limits of a small bedroom.

Modeling in N scale cuts the required space for a table layout significantly. Hollow-core doors have become popular as layout bases, and they are commonly available in 24" to 36" widths and are 6' 8" tall. Door-base layouts can be placed against a wall, which saves aisle space as well.

One disadvantage of table-style layouts is that they require sharp curves, and this can limit the types of equipment you can operate. Small

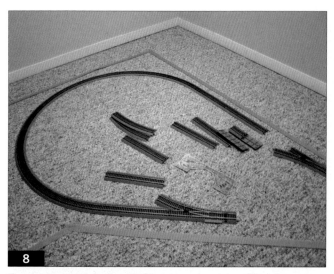

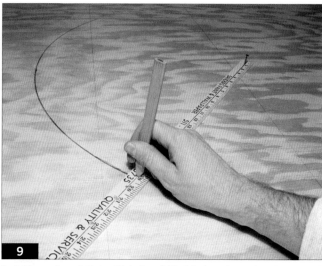

If your benchwork isn't yet built, you can tape an outline of your layout area on the floor and test track components within that space. Just be careful where you step!

An old wood yardstick with holes drilled in it makes a handy trammel for drawing accurate curves on the benchwork surface.

locomotives and short freight cars run and look better on tight curves.

Another option is a shelf or around-the-walls style layout. Shelf layouts can go all the way around a room or basement, or they can be short—just a few feet long in some cases. A layout that goes all the way around the walls will require a lift-out section, swinging gate, or duckunder at the room's access door. Shelf layouts allow you to use broader curves than do table layouts.

Small shelf layouts can be built in point-to-point style. Many modelers enjoy switching operations, and a small switching layout can feature complex trackwork but will fit on a relatively narrow shelf if there's no track loop to deal with. These layouts can also be expanded as time and space allow.

Around-the-walls layouts have become very popular because they enable what has become known as walkaround operation—where operators follow their trains as they proceed along the layout.

Although large walkaround layouts are common today, they were rare as late as the 1970s and even into the 1980s, when it was common to have operators at a central location, where they were bound to their controllers at stationary control panels. The coming of handheld DC throttles and then the advent of Digital Command Control (DCC) provided the push for this layout style.

For your first layout, a small table-style or shelf layout is ideal. Once you are comfortable with the various facets of the hobby, you can add to it or move to a larger around-the-walls layout or begin planning a basement empire.

Track planning

Once you have determined your space, the next step is to develop a track plan. The easiest way is to start with a published track plan—thousands have been published in *Model Railroader*, *Railroad Model Craftsman*, and other hobby magazines as well as in dozens of books, including *101 Track Plans for Model Railroaders* and *101 More Track Plans for Model Railroaders* (Kalmbach Books).

The term *track plan* can be deceptive, as a track plan involves a lot more than plotting the route for the rail line itself. A good example of a track plan is shown in figure **2**, a 4 x 8-foot layout based on a West Virginia coal mining area. A good track plan includes all the details of a layout, including roads, streets, structure locations, and scenic elements such as rivers and hills.

When looking at a published plan, look beyond the intentions of the designer. You can always start with the track arrangement listed and then alter the other details to suit the type of layout that you want to build. The plan may have been designed to represent a 1940s railroad in the Deep

South, but nothing says you can't change the scenery and structures to match an upper Midwestern railroad of the 1960s.

Another option is to modify a published plan or stretch it to fit a different space, **3**. You can do this by simply photocopying a plan, cutting it out, and taping it on a sheet of graph paper. Then mark your changes with a pencil. You can also combine features from multiple plans this way as long as the plans are drawn to the same scale.

You can also design your own track plan from scratch. Be aware that, although it sounds like an easy process, track planning is much trickier than simply drawing lines on a sheet of paper to represent track.

The most common mistake made by beginners (and by many experienced modelers as well) is trying to fit too much track into a plan. Turnouts take up a lot more room than you would think, and it's easy to draw several of them on a plan and discover later that they won't even come close to fitting your actual space. Sharp turnouts (nos. 4 or 5) allow the most trackwork, but broad turnouts (no. 6 or 8) will work better with long equipment—use them if space allows.

Sketching a plan freehand is a good way to get an overall idea of a design to paper, but you then need to draw an accurate plan to scale to make sure everything fits. Several companies have offered templates to help design track plans, **4**. These include turnouts in various sizes, crossings, and curves of various radii. Walthers and others offer paper templates of their track pieces, allowing you to play with various arrangements on a small scale, **5**. A compass also works well for accurately drawing curves.

For either, draw an outline of your table or area on graph paper with ink. Then use a pencil and tracing template (or paper templates) to draw the track in place. It will probably take several tries to get things the way you want them. Add outlines of other features as well, such as roads, structures, and rivers.

Track-planning software has become common in recent years. Atlas offers Right Track freeware for PCs (www. atlasrr.com). More extensive software includes 3rd PlanIt for PCs (www. trackplanning.com) and RailModeller for Macs (www.railmodeller.com). Most have premade templates for various track components, and many have templates for structures and scenic details. An advantage to these is that the track components lock together just like real pieces, avoiding the temptation to cheat a bit to squeeze in extra track.

Keep a few things in mind when planning. First, establish a minimum radius and stick to it (see sidebar at right). Don't go below the minimums listed for sharp curves, or you'll have difficulty running your trains.

Keep grades reasonable. On a small layout, grades up to 3.5 percent (3.5 units of rise for 100 units of run) are manageable; above that, you may have difficulty pulling more than a couple of cars upgrade. So, to elevate the track 3.5 feet, do it over a stretch of 100 feet of track.

Keep vertical clearance in mind if running under bridges or in tunnels; try about 22 scale feet for modern equipment from railhead to the bottom of the bridge. You can get by with less if you only run older or shorter equipment—measure your tallest car or locomotive and add a scale foot or two to be safe.

Track planning guidelines

There are few hard-and-fast rules when it comes to track planning, but these guidelines are worth keeping in mind.

- Don't pack the layout with track. Avoid the temptation to cram all the track possible into a given space. The result won't be realistic. Instead, be sure to allow room for structures and scenery.
- Include a passing siding. You'll find you'll need at least one double-ended siding (or runaround track) for either storing a train or allowing an engine to run around its train to get to the other end.
- Keep track within reach. Don't locate track more than an arm's length from the layout edge. Any table wider than 36" should have access from both sides.
- Include several spurs. Spurs are dead-end tracks that branch off the main line or a siding. These are great for placing industries and businesses and giving your trains a place to deliver freight cars.
- Add an interchange track. An interchange track is a spur that leads to the edge of a layout and serves as an imaginary connection with the outside world. This lends realism to even the smallest layouts.
- Minimize yards and engine facilities. On small layouts, keep yards to two or three tracks. Avoid turntables (they take up a lot of space) and instead use one or two spur tracks for servicing and storing locomotives.
- Allow clearance on side-by-side tracks. Keep the following minimum spacing in mind to keep cars and locomotives from sideswiping each other (test this if you have long passenger or freight cars).

Parallel track spacing (center-to-center)			
Broad curve	N	HO	O
Straight	1"	1.8"	3.5"
Sharp curve	1.4"	2.5"	4.8"
Broad curve	1.2"	2.2"	3.8"

If you're truly interested in the art of track planning, pick up a copy of John Armstrong's *Track Planning for Realistic Operation, 3rd Edition* (Kalmbach Books, 1998).

Full-size plan

It can also help to do some planning at full size. If you have a table or piece of plywood or foam handy, play with various track arrangements, **6**. Cut-out photocopies of turnouts are very handy for doing this, as are real track sections, **7**.

If you don't yet have a layout surface to work on, you can also do all of these steps directly on a hard or carpeted floor, **8**. Mark the layout outline with tape and then lay the track or templates in place. More tape can mark road locations, rivers, lakes, structures, and other layout features.

Once you have your plan in good shape, transfer it to your layout table. Marking a grid (12" or 6" squares) provides a series of good reference points. Transfer your track plan to the surface, starting with turnouts. Again, use actual or photocopied turnouts and other track sections to make sure everything fits properly.

To draw accurate curves, make a trammel with a thin piece of wood or an old wood yardstick, **9**. A small hole at the end can be placed on a nail driven into the layout surface at the center of the curve; holes drilled in the wood let you mark curves of several radii.

If you can't get a track arrangement or scene to work or look right, step away from it for awhile and then go back and try again. Sometimes taking a break will help you see things in a fresh manner. Once you have your plan ready, you can start considering benchwork.

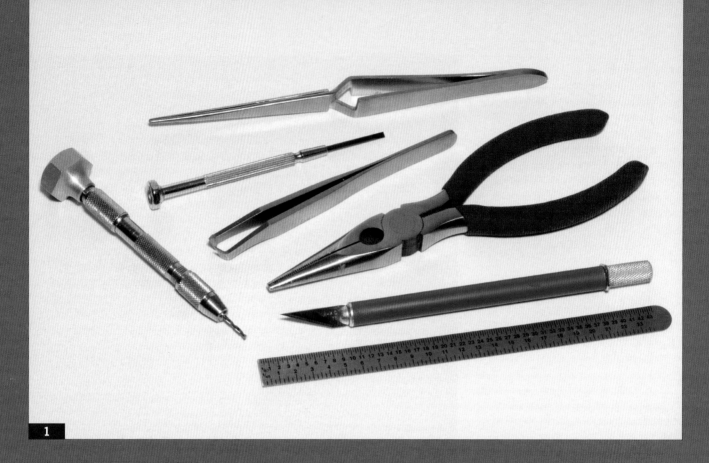

1

CHAPTER FOUR

Using tools and glues

You'll find a small collection of specialized tools to be quite handy when building and repairing models.

As you get involved in the hobby you'll discover that you need a variety of tools, 1. We'll start by looking at a basic tool kit with essential items that you'll use on most every project. After that, we'll take a look at tools that are more specialized, ones that you might want to acquire as you move on to more advanced projects.

Basic tool kit

A hobby knife will be your most-used tool, **2**. A variety of makes and handle designs are available—find one that fits your hand comfortably and then buy two of them. Why two? So you can keep a standard no. 11 blade on one handle and a flat-end (chisel-shaped) no. 17 blade on the other. You'll use the no. 11 for tasks such as cutting and scoring plastic, cleaning flash (stray material from the molding process) from plastic kit parts, removing parts from sprues, and cutting various strip and sheet materials to size. The flat-end version is good for removing plastic parts from sprues, chopping strip plastic and stripwood, and shaving and shaping plastic and resin surfaces.

A disadvantage of the no. 11 blade shape is that the fine point is prone to breaking, and once it breaks, it becomes useless for cutting and scoring. You can still keep it handy for scraping and other tasks that use the long edge, but you'll want to replace it for cutting purposes.

Replacement blades are available in bulk packs. I recommend buying a 100-count package, which brings the price down to pennies per blade. Some modelers like to sharpen and reuse old blades, but I find that to be a hassle—with new blades so inexpensive, I'd rather spend my time modeling than sharpening blades.

Be sure to properly dispose of used blades. Don't just throw them into the garbage, where they can cut you, your family members, or the garbage collector. Instead, buy a sharps disposal container (available at home improvement and hardware stores or through online vendors). You'll model for years before filling one up.

While we're talking about cutting, let's look at a work surface. Self-healing cutting mats are made in many sizes and are ideal as a primary work surface. They grip materials well while cutting, and they are easy on knife blades. They won't catch and redirect a blade accidentally as a wood surface will do once its been scored a few times.

I keep several mats handy. One stays on my workbench for all general

2

You'll use a hobby knife more than any other tool. Keep at least two handles, with chisel- and pointed-tip blades in each. Self-healing cutting mats are available in several sizes.

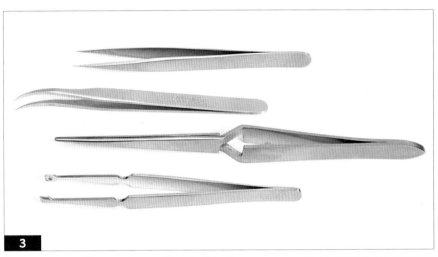

3

Tweezers come with many types of tips. Locking tweezers (second from bottom) and tweezers with indentations in the jaws (bottom) are both handy for many projects.

cutting and modeling work. The second one I save for decaling and other "clean" work. Cutting mats will eventually wear over time and acquire paint and glue splotches and other stains. Simply replace it when it no longer functions well.

Tweezers are invaluable for handling small details and positioning various parts, **3**. I keep several kinds handy. My most-used is a simple pointed-tip version. These are handy for moving parts, picking up decals, and hundreds of other jobs. Other variations include bent-tip (angled or curved) tweezers

that are handy for getting into odd spaces, and tweezers with flat ends and/or indentations in the ends, which are good for holding round parts.

Locking tweezers have points that are normally closed (sprung the opposite way of standard models), so squeezing them opens the points. These are like a helping hand when holding parts together while gluing or painting them.

You'll find clamps of various sizes and designs handy for holding parts together for gluing, fitting, and other tasks, **4**. Quick-Grip clamps are one

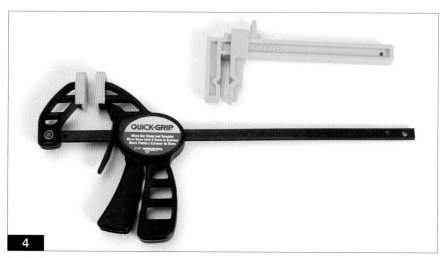

4

Small clamps, such as this X-Acto plastic version and Quick-Grip bar clamp, hold parts together during assembly and gluing.

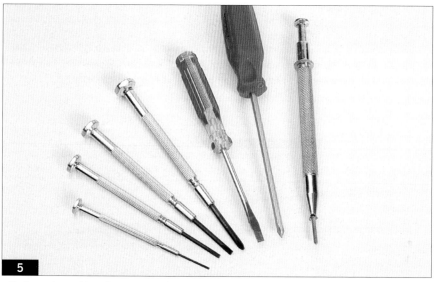

5

Various sizes of jeweler's and other small flathead and Phillips screwdrivers are needed for assembling and disassembling models. The screw picker at right has a sprung tip that holds screws securely.

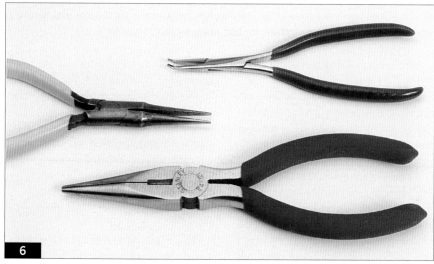

6

Various sizes of needlenose pliers are great for placing parts and grabbing details in tight spaces.

popular type; others are available from a variety of manufacturers.

You'll need screwdrivers frequently, **5**, for disassembling locomotives, assembling freight car kits, and installing and replacing couplers. Small screws are common, so you'll need a basic set of jeweler's screwdrivers with flathead and Phillips tips. You'll also need at least one additional small screwdriver of each type—larger than a jeweler's but smaller than a full-size tool.

Pliers are handy when you need to get a firm grip on a part, **6**. Needlenose pliers are especially handy for small parts and tight spaces; you can find them in straight and bent-nose versions in several sizes.

Wire cutters (also called side cutters) work for wire and brass strip material (but not steel), **7**. Specialized rail nippers are invaluable for cutting track (see Chapter 6) with a shearing action that cleanly cuts the material. Sprue cutters are flush-cutting and provide extremely clean cuts when separating plastic parts from sprues.

Pick up a couple of fine needle files in flat, round, and square or triangular shapes, **8**. You'll use them to smooth surfaces, clean openings, remove stray material from kit parts, and for many other purposes. Small sanding sticks are also handy.

A scale rule is a vital tool for any hobbyist, **9**. Many foot-long rules have markings for HO, N, O, and S scales, and rules are available for single scales as well. Clear plastic rules can be handy when taking measurements from drawings. Longer versions are also available.

Advanced tools

Much like a woodworker who gradually acquires tools as he or she completes more and more projects, most model railroaders soon discover many additional tools that make modeling tasks easier. Every modeler has a list of favorites; here are some that I find especially handy.

I'm putting it on the advanced list, but I actually consider a screw picker a necessity, **5**. It has three prongs activated by a plunger at the top of the handle for grabbing screws by the head.

You'll never again have a screw shoot across the room from the jaws of a tweezers or needlenose pliers once you have a screw picker.

A pin vise is a miniature drill, **10**. Its chuck closes all the way, and it has a swivel handle to allow you to hold it securely and turn it by hand to drill holes. With a set of nos. 61–80 bits, it is invaluable in drilling holes in plastic, resin, wood, and metal. It will be one of your first advanced tool purchases.

You'll find a couple of small squares handy for building structure kits and cutting sheet material to size, **11**. I find a small machinist's square and a common carpenter's tri-square to be the most used.

Adhesives

There's no single glue that will work well in every application, so it's vital to know what adhesives work best with different materials. With any adhesive, make sure that the joint fits tightly together, check that mating pieces are clean and free of paint, and avoid getting glue onto a finished surface.

Liquid plastic cement is almost always the best choice for plastic-to-plastic joints, **12**. This glue is a solvent that works by melting a thin layer of plastic on each surface, so the two surfaces mate and weld together. Don't try to use it with resin or for bonding plastic to another material—it simply won't work. Exercise great care when gluing clear plastic parts because stray glue will mar the clear surface.

Several types of plastic cement are available. I use two: a true liquid that must be applied with a brush (an example is Testor's no. 3502) and a gel, such as Testor's 3507, that is applied via a thin applicator tube on the bottle.

You'll find yourself using both. The liquid is designed to work by capillary action: hold two mating pieces together and then use a brush to touch liquid to the inside of the joint. Capillary action will draw the cement into the joint.

The gel works by applying it to one surface and then pressing the two mating pieces together. With both, keep the two pieces together (clamping them if possible) until the glue sets.

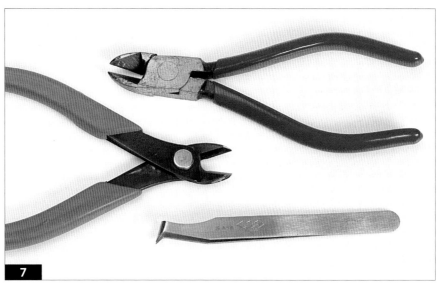

7 Standard wire cutters (top) work on copper wire and soft-metal (brass) strip materials. The Xuron rail nippers (center) uses shearing action to provide clean, square cuts on rail. The sprue cutter (bottom) is the best choice for cleanly cutting plastic parts from sprues.

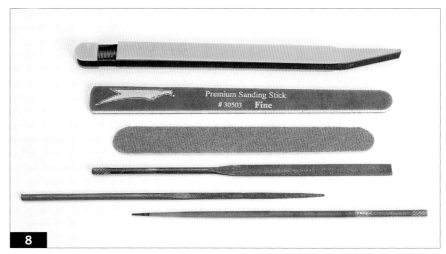

8 Shaping tools from the top: an X-Acto fine-tip sanding tool; a Squadron Products fine sanding stick; a common abrasive nail file; and flat, square, and round needle files.

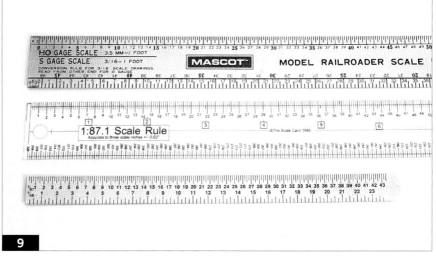

9 Scale rules include (from top) a Mascot 12" steel rule with N, HO, S, and O scale markings; a 36" clear plastic HO rule from Scale Card; and a 6" HO, O, and N scale rule from X-Acto.

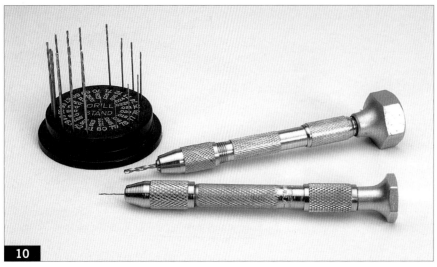

10

A pin vise is a miniature drill. Many styles are available. You'll use various drill bits in nos. 61–80 sizes frequently in model building.

11

Squares are especially handy when building structure kits. A small machinist's square and 12" carpenter's combination square both will prove useful.

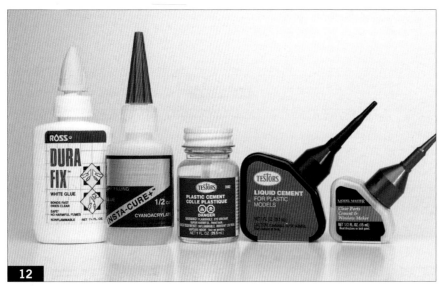

12

Common adhesives include white glue, cyanoacrylate adhesive, liquid and gel plastic cements, and clear parts glue.

You'll also find yourself frequently choosing cyanoacrylate adhesive (CA), or super glue. CA works best for joining any combination of dissimilar materials including resin, metal, wood, and plastic. It is also great for joining plastic details to a painted surface (as long as structural strength is not needed). Don't use it for gluing clear plastic as the parts can fog.

CA is made in various thicknesses, or viscosities, including thin, medium, thick, and gap-filling. Thin flows more freely than water and sets almost instantly—it can be difficult to control and is the type with which you're most likely to accidentally glue yourself to something. Thick and gap-filling varieties are more gel-like and take several seconds to set.

I use medium viscosity CA the most often, and I've found it to be the best choice for most general-purpose applications. It sets relatively quickly—within a few seconds—but it is thick enough to be easy to control. The best way to apply it is to squeeze a few drops onto a scrap piece of cardstock or plastic and apply it with a toothpick.

Thick and gap-filling CA are good for joints that are uneven. Thin is good for tight joints that can be clamped prior to application. All can be cured instantly by applying accelerator (Zip-Kicker is one brand).

Clear parts cement, such as Model Master 8876, is a good choice for gluing clear plastic or acetate windows into structures. It dries to a high gloss, which helps hide it if any remains visible after gluing.

Epoxy is good for metal or resin joints where a great deal of strength is needed or when the joint has a lot of gaps or needs reinforcement. The five-minute, two-part type works well. Make sure you use equal parts of hardener and epoxy and mix the two thoroughly.

White glue and yellow (carpenter's) glue are good for porous materials such as wood-to-wood and wood-to-cardstock joints. Don't use them with plastic, metal, or resin. White glue is fine for most applications, and yellow glue will give a stronger joint.

1

CHAPTER FIVE

Building benchwork

A solid foundation is vital when building a model railroad. There are a number of methods for building benchwork, 1, from simple tables to extensive around-the-walls supports. You don't need to be an expert woodworker to build solid benchwork, and the process is not difficult—but it does require some care and patience to get good results.

This cookie-cutter style tabletop is ready for track and scenery. The technique provides smooth, gradual grades for roadbed and roads along with level areas for structures and towns. Many techniques can be used to build benchwork, and all will work just fine as long as they provide a solid base for your layout.

2 A cordless drill is vital for drilling pilot holes and driving screws. A set of common drill bits from ¹⁄₁₆" to ⅜" and a countersinking drill bit are also handy.

3 A hand miter saw and miter box will give you square cuts on dimensional lumber.

Benchwork is a combination of a supporting structure (legs and framework) and a top surface that supports the track and scenery. The type of each that you choose will depend upon the size and type of layout you're planning. Many small layouts only need a simple table. Shelf layouts can be mounted directly on a wall, be freestanding, or be mounted atop a bookcase or other piece of furniture.

You need to consider carefully the terrain and type of scenery you plan to use, as the benchwork surface is integrated with your trackwork and scenery. For level track and gently rolling hills, a simple tabletop will work just fine. If you're planning more rugged mountain scenery, with extensive areas that will both rise above and drop below track level, an open-grid type of benchwork will be the best choice.

You'll need a few basic tools to assemble benchwork. An electric or cordless drill is invaluable for drilling holes and driving screws, **2**. A handsaw and miter box will ensure square joints (a power miter saw is even better, but don't buy one just for benchwork unless you plan to fill a basement or do other woodworking

projects), **3**. You'll also need a saber saw if you need to cut curved patterns in plywood, as with the cookie-cutter table method.

Basic tables

A simple table is ideal for a first layout. It might be tempting to just place a piece of plywood atop a pair of sawhorses. However, although ideal for a temporary setup or to play with various track designs, a sheet of plywood will flex and warp over time (especially if scenery is applied), and it won't be very stable.

A simple grid-top table can be made using 1 x 3 or 1 x 4 lumber (see sidebar on page 31 for tips on choosing lumber), **4**. An excellent option is using ½" or ¾" birch plywood, ripped to 3½" wide strips. Advantages to this are that the plywood strips are dimensionally stable, they won't warp or twist, and the overall cost will be lower. I would only do this if you already have a table saw or circular saw (although some lumberyards and home centers will make these cuts for you for a fee).

Figure **4** shows how the original layout can be expanded with an additional section. The dimensions can be adjusted to suit your needs.

Square cuts are important in keeping the table grid square and level, so use a power miter saw or miter box. Start by making the grid frame. Glue each joint with carpenter's wood glue, **5**. Drill pilot holes in the ends of the long side pieces to keep the wood from splitting and then screw the pieces in place with either flathead wood screws (no. 8 x 1¾") or 1¾" drywall screws, **6**. (If you use strips cut from ½" plywood, use 4d finishing nails.) Make sure that each joint is square and flush. Add the cross members, gluing and screwing or nailing each into place, **7**.

The legs are made from two plywood strips glued and screwed together in an L, **4** and **8**. If you do this, glue and screw a 12" length of 2 x 2 at the base of the leg. Add an adjustable foot to the bottom of each (available at lumber supply centers). Although not necessary, the feet make it easy to level the layout.

Legs can also be cut from 2 x 2s or 2 x 4s. Clamp the legs in place to the first inbound crosspiece so that each is set 6" inside the edge of the frame. Secure the legs with bolts instead of screws. This will allow you to easily remove the legs later if you need to move the layout. Drill a ¼" hole

Table construction

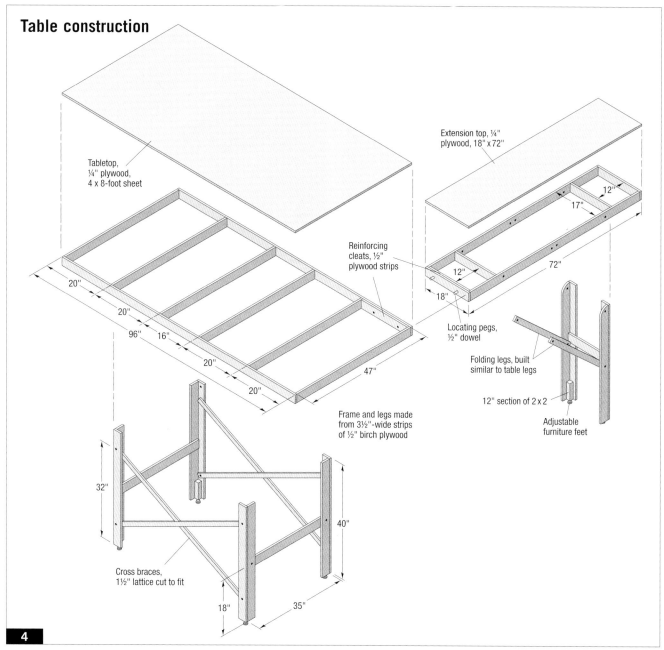

Tabletop,
¼" plywood,
4 x 8-foot sheet

Extension top, ¼"
plywood, 18" x 72"

Reinforcing
cleats, ½"
plywood strips

12"

17"

12"

72"

18"

Locating pegs,
½" dowel

Folding legs, built
similar to table legs

12" section of 2 x 2

Adjustable
furniture feet

20"

20"

96" 16"

20"

47"

20"

Frame and legs made
from 3½"-wide strips
of ½" birch plywood

32"

40"

Cross braces,
1½" lattice cut to fit

18" 35"

4

This simple grid-top table will work for most table layouts. The size can be adjusted to suit your available space and needs.

5

Glue wood joints with carpenter's (yellow) wood glue.

6

Use wood or drywall screws to fasten joints. Pilot holes will keep
lumber from splitting.

7 Here's the finished table frame grid—this one is built from 1 x 4 dimensional lumber. The legs can now be installed.

8 Add a 12" length of 2 x 2 inside the L-shaped legs. The adjustable foot (a bolt inside of a T-nut) is optional but makes it easy to level the layout.

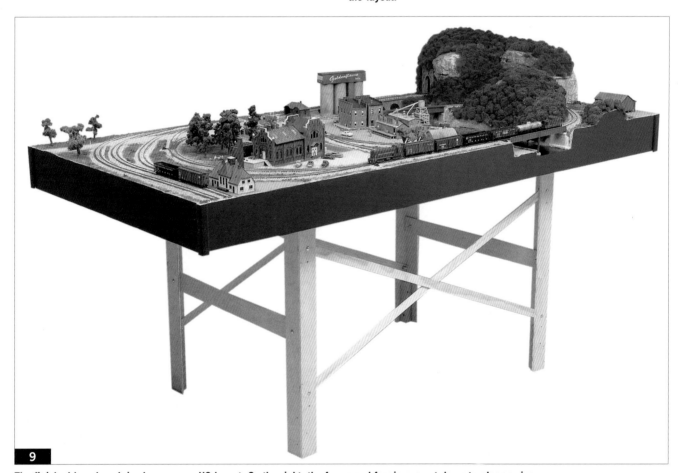

9 The finished benchwork is shown on an HO layout. On the right, the frame and fascia are cut down to clear a river.

through the crosspiece and leg and secure it with a ¼" x 3" bolt and nut (with washers on both sides).

Fasten the angled braces in place with screws, but don't glue them. This will make it easier to remove them if the layout needs to be moved.

Figure 4 shows legs that are 40" long, but layout height is largely a matter of preference. Shorter legs (36"–40") are fine if you plan to run the layout while seated, and many layouts that feature walkaround operation are 48" or taller. You can see a finished

layout on the benchwork in photo **9**.

A variation on the grid table is L-girder benchwork, **10**. This relies on two pairs of legs to support a pair of L-shaped girders, each made from a 1 x 2 glued and screwed atop a 1 x 3 or 1 x 4. Figure **11** provides details.

Lumber basics

Dimensional lumber and plywood are the most common benchwork materials. Lumber is available in several common sizes, including 1 x 2, 1 x 3, 1 x 4, 2 x 2, and 2 x 4. Note the lack of inch marks: dimensional lumber is actually smaller than its indicators, because all sides have been planed smooth. Thus, a 1 x 2 is actually ¾" x 1½", a 2 x 4 is 1½" x 3½", and so on.

Plywood is made of several layers of wood veneer glued to each other with the grain of each layer at right angles. This makes plywood strong and resistant to shrinking or expanding because of temperature and humidity changes. Common thicknesses range from ¼" to ¾" in ⅛" increments.

For layout surfaces, ½" is fine for a solid table, but I recommend ⅝" if you plan to cut it into narrow pieces (such as with the cookie-cutter method). Thinner plywood (¼" and ⅜") tends to sag in many benchwork applications. Thin plywood is fine for backdrops, control panels, and small support shelves. Heavy (¾") plywood can be cut into strips and substituted for 1 x 2, 1 x 3, and 1 x 4 lumber.

When buying lumber for benchwork, remember that most of it will eventually be covered by scenery. Softwood (pine or fir) is fine for benchwork. When selecting, choose kiln-dried, untreated wood.

Dimensional lumber is graded by quality. The best is select (or select structural), which is free of knots, followed by no. 1, no. 2, and no. 3, which allow progressively larger knots and imperfections. (Nos. 1 and 2 are generally grouped together and sold as "no. 2 and better.") Don't waste money on cabinet-grade lumber when you don't have to—select lumber can be many times more expensive than no. 2.

The most important quality for benchwork lumber is that it should be straight and free of twists. Small knots won't disrupt construction, but make sure knots don't take up more than a quarter of the width of a board. Slight bowing or cupping is permissible but avoid twisted boards—these will throw everything out of alignment. Ensure the quality of your lumber by choosing your own boards at a lumberyard or home center.

Plywood is also graded but with a different scale. Each surface is given a grade of A, B, C, or D with A the best (sanded with knots plugged) down to D (rough). For most benchwork uses, A-C or B-C plywood does well.

Avoid particleboard, which is a heavy, dense material made by bonding sawdust and glue at high pressure and temperature. This material is difficult to cut, very hard (making it difficult to drive nails and fasteners into it), and more prone to sagging than plywood. Also avoid OSB (waferboard and strandboard). Designed as sheathing, the surface of OSB is generally too rough to work well as a benchwork surface.

Tempered hardboard (Masonite is one brand) is a thin, high-density fiberboard that has a smooth, hard surface on one or both sides. It is often used as a backdrop or for making control panels and fascias.

10

L-girder benchwork features a series of 1 x 3 or 1 x 4 joists laid across two long L-shaped girders. This is a 4 x 8-foot table, but the design can be stretched up to 14 feet using just four legs.

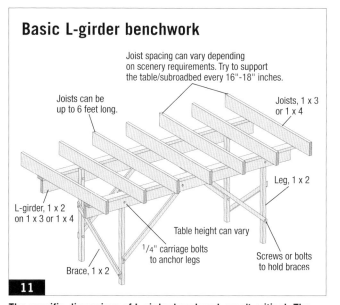

Basic L-girder benchwork

Joist spacing can vary depending on scenery requirements. Try to support the table/subroadbed every 16"-18" inches.

Joists can be up to 6 feet long.

Joists, 1 x 3 or 1 x 4

Leg, 1 x 2

L-girder, 1 x 2 on 1 x 3 or 1 x 4

Table height can vary

¼" carriage bolts to anchor legs

Screws or bolts to hold braces

Brace, 1 x 2

11

The specific dimensions of L-girder benchwork aren't critical. The girders should be spaced about ⅗ as wide as the joist length.

The L-girder design works for tables up to 14 feet long with just two pairs of legs. It's greatest strength is flexibility: it's easy to adjust the spac-ing, length, angle, and position of the crosswise joists to suit your needs for table width and below-table features such as lakes, rivers, and valleys.

The 1 x 3 or 1 x 4 joists are secured by running screws up through the flange on the L-girder into the joist. The joists can be up

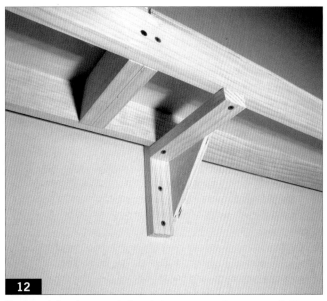

12

13

Commercial or homemade brackets can support a narrow shelf layout. This pair of 1 x 2s with a small plywood bracket holds a 12"-wide section of layout. *Jim Forbes*

Wider benchwork grids can be anchored to the wall with an angled bracket from the base of the wall to the edge of the frame. This 1 x 2 is anchored to a short 2 x 2 screwed to the wall into a stud.

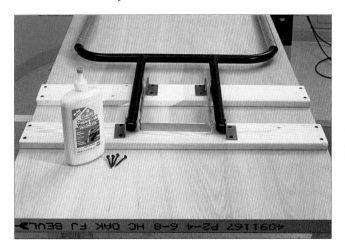

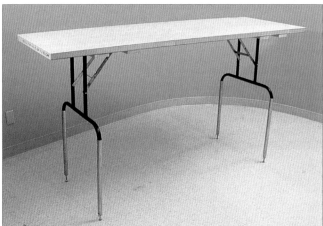

14

To add folding legs to a hollow-core door, mount two 1 x 4s to the door, screwing them into the door's frame (top left photo). The legs can then be secured to the 1 x 4s. These legs have been extended by fitting them into lengths of metal conduit attached by screws. *Jim Forbes photos*

15

Mark the areas that require cutting and use a saber saw to cut along the lines. Make sure you don't accidentally cut the joists or frame.

16

After the plywood is cut, use risers to elevate the plywood to the desired height.

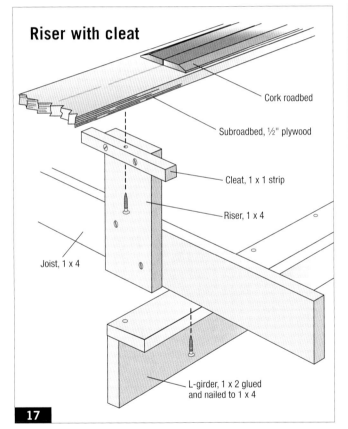

Riser with cleat

Cork roadbed

Subroadbed, ½" plywood

Cleat, 1 x 1 strip

Riser, 1 x 4

Joist, 1 x 4

L-girder, 1 x 2 glued and nailed to 1 x 4

17

18

This open-grid benchwork still has track on plywood subroadbed. The open grid will eventually be covered by hilly scenery, so a table surface is unnecessary.

to 6 feet wide if needed with one set of girders. Make the girder spacing about 7" wider for each additional 12" of joist width.

If your space allows it, you can anchor benchwork to a wall. For narrow shelves (up to 18" or so), small commercial or homemade shelf brackets can be used to support foam, plywood, or a light grid, **12**. For wider layouts (up to 30" or so), a V-shaped bracket will support a grid-style or plain table layout top, **13**. Shelves wider than 30" aren't recommended because it gets very difficult to reach into the back of a scene.

Make sure any brackets anchored to a wall are fastened securely into wall studs. Screws must be long enough so at least 1½" of the screw extends into the stud (allow for the thickness of paneling, drywall, and other materi-

als). If the screws go into just the wall material without hitting a stud, they will pull out easily.

Hollow-core-door table

An easy-to-build option for small layouts (especially for N scale) is to use a hollow-core door as a table. These doors are a made from two pieces of thin plywood on a narrow wood frame that goes around the edge. Hollow-core

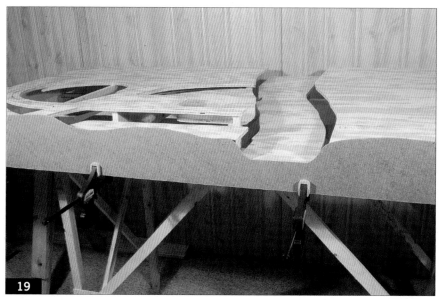

19

Fascia provides a clean appearance for the front of the layout. This is tempered hardboard with the profile cut to match the future scenery. It can be secured with wood glue and then clamped in place. Wood screws with finishing washers can also be used.

20

While most fascias are painted black or brown, Rick Rideout painted the fascia deep green on his HO Louisville & Nashville layout to match the scenery. *Rick Rideout*

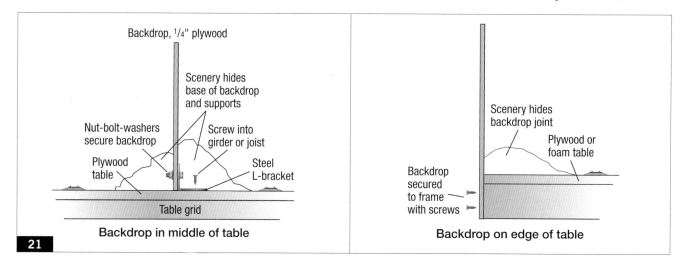

21

doors are lightweight but much more stable than a simple piece of plywood. Add a pair of folding or permanent legs (available at home centers), **14**, and you're ready to go. Hollow-core doors can also easily be mounted atop a bookcase, wall brackets, or a wall shelf.

Be sure to anchor all connections to the outside edges of the door as the photos show, as the only solid area is the narrow wood frame around the edges.

Cookie-cutter top

You can lay track and build scenery directly atop a flat tabletop. However, if you want to vary the elevation of the track and add scenic elements below

track level, consider the cookie-cutter method, **1** and **15**. This technique has been around since the beginning of the hobby because it is versatile, easy to do, provides a solid base for track and scenery, and works well.

Start with a sheet of ½" or ⅝" plywood. Don't yet anchor it to the table. Mark the track locations on it, along with the locations of scenic elements such as lakes, rivers, structures, and roads (described in Chapter 3). Determine the areas that will need to be raised or lowered, mark lines for cutting, and cut along the lines with a saber saw.

Elevated areas must be supported above the table grid by risers—short

lengths of 1 x 2s, 1 x 3s, or 1 x 4s, **16**. The traditional way to do this is with cleats, **17**. Although a bit more work, attaching the riser via a cleat allows the riser to be easily moved in the future if changes are necessary. If you plan to use under-table switch machines, make sure you don't add a riser directly below a turnout throw-bar location.

You can also simply attach the plywood to the riser with a screw from above. Make sure the screwheads are countersunk below the plywood surface to ensure a smooth path for roadbed. If a riser needs to be moved, remove the screws holding it to the joist and either cut it away or just leave it hanging in place.

22

Don Culp's 2'-6" x 5'-0" N scale Great Northern layout rests on simple open-grid benchwork with 2 x 2 legs. The backdrop at the rear is a combination of painted-on details and cut-out structures. The fascia is notched for a river, and the fascia also supports a power pack and small control panel. *Don Culp*

A variation on the cookie-cutter method is open-grid benchwork, **18**. With this, the only plywood surface is the track roadbed itself. This is good for mountainous and other rugged scenery where there's no real need for a table surface. You can still add plywood where needed, such as under rivers, roads, and structures. Make the grid top the lowest level of scenery (such as a lake or river) and elevate everything else from there.

Building more-extensive benchwork is simply a matter of connecting the above benchwork types over a larger area. You can simply join tables and grids together. Mix open-grid and cookie-cutter benchwork as needed: open-grid through a mountainous area and cookie-cutter as the track enters a town or city area.

Plywood isn't your only option for a layout surface. Extruded polystyrene foam (the blue or pink sheets sold as insulation) comes in thicknesses from ½" to 2". It can be cut and elevated like plywood or layered to create scenic effects above and below track level. Woodland Scenics' foam risers can also be used to create track elevations on a flat table. See Chapter 9 for samples.

Fascia

The fascia is simply a cover for the front of the layout. It hides the edges of the scenery and benchwork frame and provides a neat appearance as well as a place for control panels, switches, and other devices.

Hardboard (such as Masonite) is a popular choice for a fascia since it is sturdy, it takes paint well, and the ⅛" variety is relatively easy to bend into curves. Thin plywood also works well, provided no bending is required. The fascia should extend enough above the table level, so it can follow the contour of the scenery at the edge of the layout, **19**.

The easiest way to secure the fascia is with wood screws and finishing washers. For a clean appearance, you can use screws countersunk below the fascia surface and cover the screwheads with putty.

Most modelers paint fascia a dark color, usually black or brown or a deep green to match surrounding scenery, **20**.

Backdrop

A backdrop—even a simple sky-blue board—is a huge improvement over a basement wall or room wall as a background for your layout, **20**. The backdrop board itself should be in place before the track and scenery.

For small layouts, thin plywood (¼") is a great backdrop choice. When cut to a 24" to 30" width, the plywood is strong enough that it can be fastened to the benchwork at its base with no other framework needed, **21**. For a backdrop at the rear of benchwork that will be seen on only one side, use A-C grade; if both sides will be seen, choose A-A grade. To fasten a backdrop down the center of a layout, use steel L-brackets (available at hardware stores) fastened to the backdrop and the table or joists. These can be hidden later with scenery.

Tempered hardboard (such as Masonite) is also a popular choice for backdrops. You can use ⅛"-thick material, but it will require additional bracing. The ¼" variety is stronger and can be used like plywood.

A finished small table-style layout with a backdrop can be seen in **22**.

This should get you well on your way to providing a firm foundation for a layout. You'll find many more details on the specifics of construction in *Basic Model Railroad Benchwork* (Kalmbach Books, 2002).

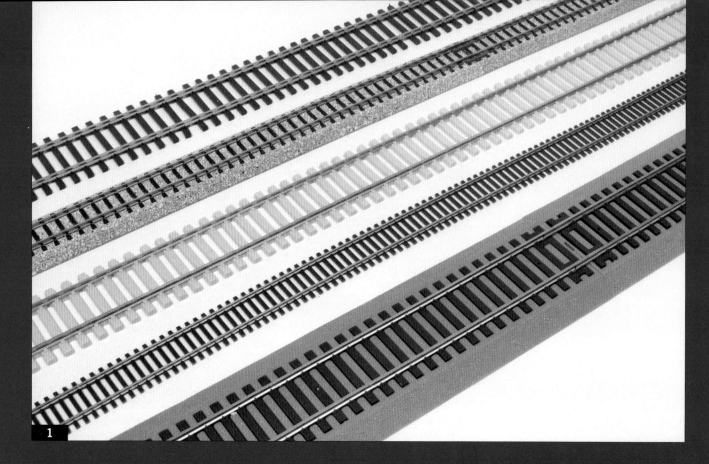

1

CHAPTER SIX

Laying track and roadbed

Many types of model track are available, including traditional standard sectional and flextrack sections as well as all-in-one track featuring roadbed. From the top: Walthers HO code 83 flextrack, Kato N scale Unitrack, Atlas HO code 83 flextrack with concrete ties, Atlas N code 55 flextrack, and Atlas HO True-Track.

Installing track properly is critical to smooth, trouble-free operation. Track, roadbed, and ballast also serve as important scenic elements in creating a realistic model railroad. You have many choices in track types and construction methods, 1. Let's start with a look at real track.

Prototype track and roadbed

Real track has several elements, **2**. A train's steel wheels ride on a pair of steel rails with a gauge (separation) of 4'-8½". The rails are held securely in alignment by crossties (or simply ties) of wood or concrete. Steel tie plates sit between the rail and tie, keeping the rail from damaging the tie.

Wood ties are the most common, with the rails spiked to the ties. The past 20 years have seen an increase in the use of concrete ties, mostly on heavy-traffic main lines, **3**. Concrete ties have a different shape (usually dipping to a thinner profile between rails) and use clips instead of spikes to hold rails in place.

Real track features either jointed or welded rail. Most track on secondary and branch lines, as well as sidings and spurs, is jointed. Short lengths of rail connect end-to-end with joint bars keeping them attached and aligned. Most of these rail sections are 39 feet long, although recent installations have featured longer rail lengths.

Welded rail (also called ribbon rail) grew in popularity starting in the late steam era, especially for high-traffic main lines. Short lengths of rail are welded end-to-end (at the manufacturer or on-site) to form long stretches of rail with no joints. The result is smoother operation, without the wear caused by wheels battering the ends of rails at conventional joints.

The ties rest on a bed of crushed rock called ballast. This keeps the track level and aligned and provides for drainage. Ballast thickness varies, with up to 12" common for main lines and 6" to 8" for sidings and secondary tracks. Industrial spurs often have little or no ballast. During the steam era, they rested on a bed of cinders.

The ballast, in turn, is laid on a graded subroadbed. This provides a level area for the track, with ditches on each side to provide for drainage.

The appearance of track and roadbed varies: a main line that sees a dozen or more trains a day will have a very clean, well-maintained profile, and a branch or secondary line that hosts a few trains a week might have an undulating profile, uneven rails, and weeds sprouting through the ballast. Some

2 Prototype track features steel rails on wood or concrete ties. The near two spur tracks feature jointed rail, while the rear mainline and passing siding tracks are welded (ribbon) rail.

3 Concrete ties have become common on heavy-traffic main lines. Note the clips (instead of standard spikes) holding the rails in place and the ballast covering the ties where their profile becomes thinner in the middle.

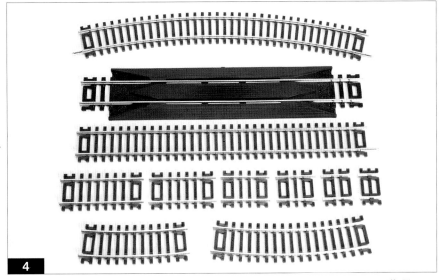

4 Sectional track includes rigid straight and curved pieces in various lengths and radii. These are from the Atlas HO scale code 83 line; the rerailer (second from top) is Atlas code 100.

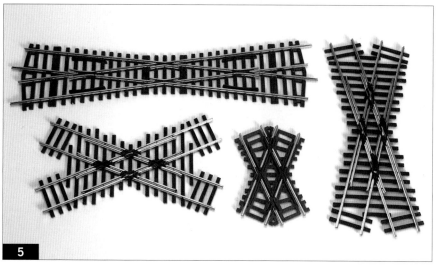

5

Crossings are made in many angles. These HO pieces include (clockwise from top left): Atlas 19 degree, Walthers 30 degree, Atlas 45 degree, and Walthers 45 degree.

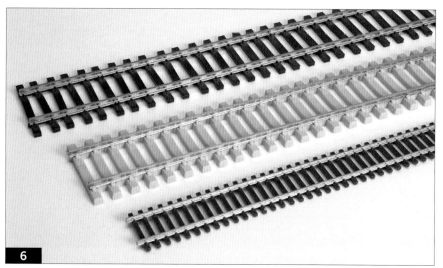

6

This selection of flextrack includes (from top) Walthers/Shinohara HO code 83, Atlas HO code 83 with concrete ties, and Atlas N scale code 55.

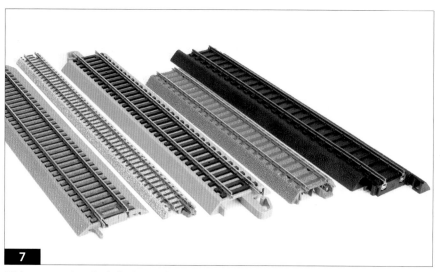

7

All-in-one sections include the track as well as roadbed with simulated ballast. From left are Atlas HO True-Track, Kato N scale Unitrack, Bachmann HO E-Z Track, Trix HO C Track, and Life-Like HO Power-Loc track.

seldom-used spur and siding tracks are overgrown with weeds, which makes it difficult to see the rails.

Passing sidings are double-ended tracks next to a main track, so trains can get by each other. Spurs are single-ended (stub) tracks, generally used as industrial sidings or storage tracks.

Types of model track

Scale track falls into three categories: sectional, flextrack, and handlaid. Sectional track is what it sounds like, individual pieces of track (ties and rail joined together) in standard lengths, **4**. Sizes vary by scale: in HO, a standard length of straight track is 9"; in N scale, 6"; and O scale, 10". To make for easier fits, other lengths are also available.

Curved sections are named by the radius. The most-common sectional track radius in HO is 18", 9¾" in N, and 36" in O scale. These curves are all considered to be sharp, so most manufacturers offer broader curves as well, including 22" in HO, 11" in N, and 40½" in O. The number of curved pieces needed to form a complete circle varies with the radius and the scale; for example, it takes 12 standard 18"-radius HO sections to make a circle. Many additional sizes are offered, so it is easy to join track into various configurations. Sectional track also includes many specialty track pieces, such as turnouts and crossings, **5**.

Flextrack comes in longer sections, generally three feet or one meter in length, **6**. As its name implies, flextrack can be bent to almost any radius curve. The longer sizes also mean fewer rail joints. It's the track of choice for most experienced modelers, who combine it with standard sectional turnouts and crossings.

The main disadvantage of flextrack is that it must be cut to fit. Every time a piece is curved, one rail becomes longer than the other, which requires the rail to be trimmed to fit.

Handlaid track involves fastening rails to individual ties in much the same way real track is laid. The process is beyond the scope of this book, but some experienced modelers prefer this method, feeling that it provides the most realistic appearance.

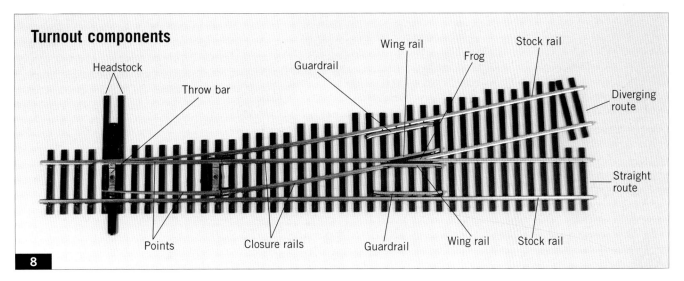

Turnout components

Headstock
Throw bar
Guardrail
Wing rail
Frog
Stock rail
Diverging route
Straight route
Points
Closure rails
Guardrail
Wing rail
Stock rail

8

All-in-one

Many manufacturers now offer sectional track that's combined with injection-molded roadbed, **7**. This roadbed is molded in gray or black (or in multiple colors) with texture to represent the rock ballast of real railroads. Some lines have the roadbed molded with the ties; others are separate, with the track attached to the roadbed.

These products include Atlas True-Track (HO, N), Bachmann E-Z Track (HO, N), Kato Unitrack (HO, N), Life-Like Power-Loc (HO, N), Micro-Trains Micro-Track (Z), and Trix C (HO). Unlike standard sectional track, each of these lines use their own proprietary method of connecting track sections, so one manufacturer's track isn't compatible with any other.

This type of track has a couple of advantages. First, it's stable. Connectors generally snap together securely with some type of locking action, unlike the plain slide-in-place rail joiners of standard track, so it will stay together better. Also, all-in-one track avoids the need for using separate roadbed and ballast as you need to do with traditional track.

Disadvantages include expense: all-in-one track costs more than standard track (although the disparity isn't as bad when you add the costs of separate roadbed and ballast). Its appearance is also a factor, as it's difficult to beat the more realistic look of rock ballast added to conventional roadbed. Also, there's no flextrack option for

9

A wye turnout has no straight route—the two routes curve away from each other.

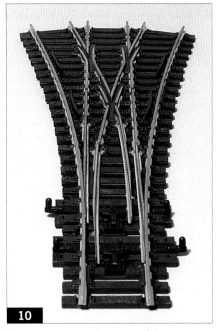

10

Three-way turnouts have a straight route as well as a curved route to each side.

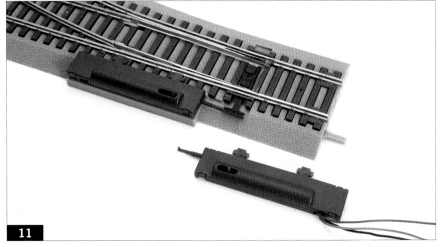

11

This Atlas HO True-Track turnout has a manual controller attached to its side. The remote-control version has an electric switch machine in the same housing.

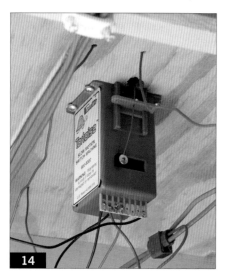

12

Caboose ground throws are mounted next to the turnout throw bar. Flipping the handle moves the throw bar, which shifts the points to the other route.

13

To make a turnout spring, drill a hole in the center tie near the throw bar. Bend a steel wire as shown (above left) and fit it into the holes. Adjust the angle of the bend in the middle so that the wire holds the turnout in each position when moved.

14

Tortoise switch machines are popular for under-table installation. Screws hold the machine to the table, and the control wire passes through the table and roadbed into a hole in the turnout throw bar. Be sure to drill the access hole before laying the turnout.

all-in-one track. You're limited to the rather tight curves offered in each line.

All-in-one track is not a bad option for small layouts. However, for larger layouts where more curve options are needed, traditional track is usually the better choice.

Turnouts and crossings

Turnouts, or switches, allow a train to change routes from one track to another. Standard turnouts have a straight route and a curved (diverging) route and are known as left- or right-hand turnouts depending on the direction of the diverging track.

The parts of a turnout, **8**, include the points (the moving rails that shift wheels from one route to another), frog (the point where the inside rails of each route come together), guardrails, wing rails, stock rails, and closure rails.

Turnout size is usually indicated by a number that indicates the sharpness of the angle of the diverging route. For example, on a no. 5 turnout, the track travels five units of length for one unit of separation. The lower the number, the sharper the turnout; the higher the number, the broader the turnout.

With numbered turnouts, the diverging route curves from the main route and passes straight through the frog. Some model turnouts (such as Atlas Snap-Switches) have a diverging route that curves through the frog, enabling it to match a standard curved piece of sectional track. With these turnouts, the size is indicated by the radius of the diverging route.

Other types of turnouts include a wye turnout, where both routes curve away from each other, **9**. Curved turnouts have both routes curving in the same direction. They are listed by the radius of each route. Three-way turnouts have a straight route plus a diverging route to each side, **10**.

Crossings allow tracks to cross but not change routes. They are listed by the angle (in degrees) that the tracks meet. Most manufacturers offer crossings at 90- and 45-degree angles, and others feature additional crossings such as 60-, 30-, and 19-degree pieces.

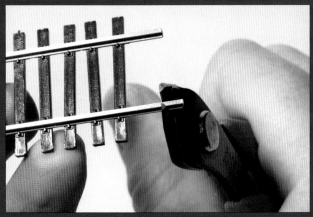 

A Xuron rail cutter is quick and easy to use. It provides a clean cut rail, and any burrs on the cut edge can be removed with a fine mill file.

My favorite track-cutting tool is a Xuron rail nipper (described in Chapter 4). Rail cutters should be among your first tool purchases when you decide to build a layout. The Xuron nippers use a shearing action, unlike standard wire cutters. This type of cut leaves a very clean edge on the end of the rail being cut.

Mark the rail to be cut with a fine-point permanent marker and use the nippers to cut the rail at the mark. A fine flat mill file will quickly clean up any jagged edges or burrs on the rail end.

Don't use these cutters for steel rail, steel wire (such as piano wire), stainless steel parts, sprues, or any other material. Steel items in particular will damage the blades, making it impossible to get a clean cut in rail.

You could also use a motor tool with a cutoff disk, such as those from Dremel, but it can be dangerous to hold the rail while trying to cut it, and clamping the track can be a hassle. I find handheld cutters to be easier, faster, and more accurate.

Another option is a razor saw. This tool works just fine, but using it is time consuming and tedious when making more than one or two cuts.

Whichever method you choose, be sure to always wear eye protection when cutting any kind of rail. Little bits of metal can go flying during the process, and a trip to the emergency room is never a good way to conclude a session of modeling.

Turnout control

You'll need a means of controlling (or throwing) each turnout. Real switches are controlled either at the switch by manually turning a lever on a switch stand or remotely by the dispatcher using a powered switch machine.

Likewise, model turnouts are either manual or remote-control. Manual turnouts require a mechanism at the turnout itself to throw it and hold the points in position. Some turnouts have this built-in; for others, you'll need to supply the mechanism.

Remote-control turnouts have an electric switch machine installed on the side of the turnout, **11**. These must be wired to a power supply and controller that allows the turnout to be thrown from a remote location.

These are handy, easy to install, and usually work well, but they have one big disadvantage: appearance. The side-mounted switch machines just aren't

very realistic. For this reason, most experienced modelers buy manual turnouts and then add either manual switch stands or switch machines that can be hidden below the track and benchwork.

For a small layout where turnouts are within easy reach, or even on large layouts where the engineer is following his or her train, manual turnouts are often a good choice. Caboose Industries is one popular line of ground throws, **12**.

Some turnouts have internal springs that snap the points in position, so no switch stand is needed—an operator need only slide the points over by hand. You can also make your own springs to do this, **13**.

Experienced modelers often opt for under-table switch machines, **14**. Several types of powered switch machines are available. They work on the same principle, with a moving lever that pivots a wire that, in turn, moves the throw bar back and forth. Specific installation

varies from model to model, but they are screwed in place on the underside of the table.

All require a power supply and a method of controlling them (see Chapter 7). You don't have to decide right away whether to choose under-table machines, but if you think you may want to eventually add them, drill an access hole for the control wire under the turnout throw bar before installing the turnout.

Rail size and material

Track in each scale comes with different sizes, or heights, of rail. Regardless of scale, rail height is measured in terms of "code," which simply refers to its height in thousandths of an inch. For example, rail that's .083" tall (83 thousandths of an inch) is code 83.

If you're shopping for track in HO scale, you'll find three common sizes: code 100, code 83, and code 70. Code

15

16

Popular roadbed choices include one-piece Woodland Scenics Track-Bed (left), which is a light foam material, and two-piece cork. These are HO scale examples, but the products are available in N and O scales as well.

Cork roadbed comes in 36"-long strips, perforated down the middle at an angle. Peeling the halves apart provides two pieces, each beveled on one side.

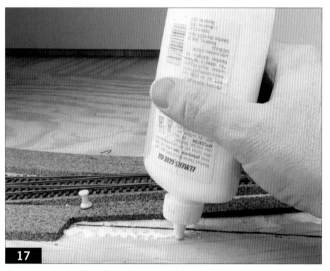

17

Run a bead of white glue along one side of the track center line and then press a section of cork roadbed into place. Push pins or tacks will hold it in place until the glue dries. Stagger the end joints between the roadbed sections.

18

19

For roadbed under turnouts, simply cut the inner cork sections to fit. A precise fit is not necessary—ballast will soon cover up the joints.

One-piece cork pads are available for turnouts and crossings. This HO turnout piece is from Midwest Products.

20

Go over the top shoulder of the cork with a sanding block to get rid of the small ridge (right) that remains after separating the sections.

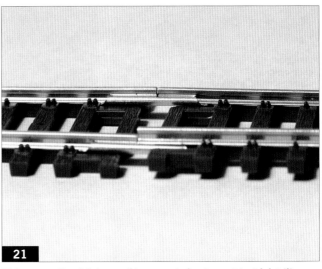

21

Make sure all rail joiners slide properly in place. A bad joint like this one will cause derailments.

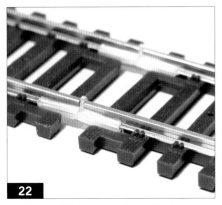

22

Insulated rail joiners, made of plastic, separate rails into blocks for wiring purposes. These HO joiners are from Atlas. You may have to trim them slightly to match the height of the rail.

23

Terminal rail joiners eliminate the need for soldering feeder wires to rails. Drill an access hole below the joint so the wire can pass through the benchwork. It will be hidden by ballast later.

24

Tap the track nail to just above rail height with a small hammer. Don't try to drive the nail all the way into place, or you could damage the rails or ties.

100 was once the most popular height and is still common in train-set quality track, but it is actually quite oversize compared to real rail. Code 83 more closely matches the size of rail used on main lines of real railroads, with code 70 representing lighter-duty track.

In N scale, code 80 track is the traditional size, but it is too tall to accurately represent real rail. Code 55 is a much better choice for a realistic appearance.

All of this might seem insignificant or picky as you enter the hobby, but as you gain experience, your eye will begin to discern subtle scale differences. Start out with proper rail sizes, and you won't regret the choice.

Rail on most model track today is made from nickel-silver. Brass was a common rail material into the 1980s, but fell out of favor because the oxidation that forms on unused track is nonconductive. This means brass rail requires more frequent cleaning than nickel-silver rail.

Some sectional track lines have used steel rail. I recommend avoiding this—it's impossible to solder rail joints or solder track feeders to it, and modifying it (such as cutting a section to fit) is difficult.

Roadbed

Although it's possible to lay your track directly on the layout table or surface, it will be much more realistic if you mount it atop roadbed, **15**. Several types of roadbed are available. Historically the most popular has been cork roadbed.

It's inexpensive, easy to work with, and readily available in all scales, **16**.

Cork comes in 36"-long strips, perforated down the middle with a bevel. Peeling the halves apart and flipping one half over provides roadbed with a slope on each side. Cork is also available in large sheets, handy for yards or complex track situations such as junctions.

To lay cork roadbed, you'll need the track center line marked on the layout surface. If using a wood tabletop, glue cork in place with common white glue, and if you're using it atop extruded foam, use Woodland Scenics Foam Tack Glue or Liquid Nails for Projects.

Spread glue along one side of the center line, **17**, and lay one half of the cork, pressing it in place along the

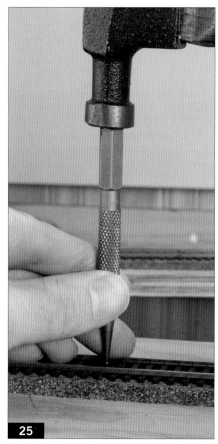

25

Several small taps on a nail set will drive the nail to just above tie-top level.

26

There should be a paper-thin gap between the nail and tie—don't drive the nail too far, or the tie will bend.

27

Press the spike in place through the mounting hole and into the roadbed with needlenose pliers. Angle the spike slightly toward the rail.

center line. Push pins or small wire nails will hold it in place (these can be removed when the glue dries). Staggering the joints on each side provides a smoother surface for the track.

Roadbed under turnouts can be easily formed by cutting the cork to fit, **18**. Lay the outside strips first, then use a hobby knife to cut each inside strip to fit as needed (the fit need not be precise). Midwest and other companies also make one-piece cork pads sized to fit under turnouts, **19**.

Once the glue has dried, go over the top surface and edges of the roadbed with a sanding block and sandpaper (120-grit or so). This will get rid of any ridges where the cork strip is separated, **20**.

Another popular roadbed in HO, N, and O scales is Woodland Scenics Track-Bed. This is a one-piece soft foam roadbed that comes in both strips and rolls. To ensure proper alignment, you might find it handy to draw a line at one of the outside edges of the roadbed.

Lay Track-Bed in similar fashion as cork, by spreading a thin layer of glue and pressing it into place. You might need to pin curves in place until the glue sets. Cut and shape turnout locations as done with cork roadbed. Large sheets of Track-Bed are also available.

Laying track

There are several worthy methods of laying track, including glue, nails, and track spikes. Whichever method you choose, it's vital that you test-fit the track before securing it. Then, as you lay the track, make sure each piece aligns properly with the preceding piece and ensure that the rail joiners fit properly, **21**. The rails should fit firmly against each other.

Also at this time, make sure you add insulated rail joiners, **22**, and track-feeder rail joiners, **23**, if you choose to use them, at the proper locations. See Chapter 7 for more information on wiring. Also, if you plan to install under-table switch machines, make sure you drill the appropriate access

holes under the turnout throw bar locations.

The traditional method of securing track in most scales—and one that works well if you have a wood table or subroadbed—is with nails or track spikes. Most sectional track has small holes in the middle of several ties (usually at each end and the middle) for track nails. Atlas and others sell small nails specifically for this, with a thin profile and small rounded head. The nails are black to blend into the ties.

Start at a turnout or complex trackwork area. Have the track pieces connected so they align properly with the roadbed. Use needlenose pliers to push a track nail into the hole and through the roadbed and then use a small hammer to start tapping it in place, **24**. Finish driving the nail with a nail set, **25**. Leave a small gap between the nail head and tie, **26**. Driving the nail farther can distort the tie and kink the track. If you accidentally bend or kink a nail, pull it out (a wire cutter is handy for this) and redo it with a new one.

28

Use the tip of the pliers to push the spike the rest of the way against the base of the rail.

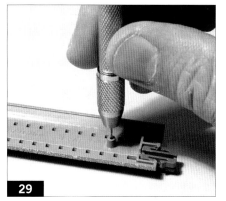

29

Some types of all-in-one track, such as the Kato N Unitrack at left, require drilling pilot holes for track nails. The track can be secured by nails as done with standard sectional track (right).

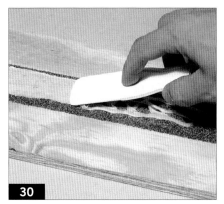

30

Run a narrow bead of adhesive down the center of the roadbed and use a putty knife to spread it into a thin layer.

31

Press the track firmly into place on the adhesive. When the glue dries, the track will be held firmly in place.

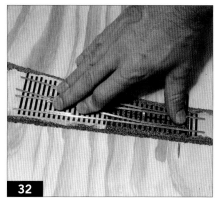

32

When gluing turnouts, don't spread adhesive under the throw bar or points.

Add another track section and repeat the process, making sure the track stays aligned as you proceed.

Instead of having holes in the middle of ties, some brands of HO and larger track have holes for spikes next to the rails. This looks more realistic, but it requires a different technique. For starters, use scale track spikes (available from Micro Engineering, Walthers, and others) that have a square profile and a spike head resembling real spikes.

Use a needlenose pliers to start the spike and push it as far as possible into the mounting hole, **27**. Close the jaws and use the tip of the pliers to push the spike the rest of the way into place, **28**. The spike must go through the roadbed and penetrate partially into the wood subroadbed for adequate holding power.

Occasionally, a spike will kink or bend over. Pull it out and substitute a new spike. If the wood is too hard to press the spikes into place, drill a small pilot hole with a pin vise before adding the spike.

All-in-one track can be secured with nails in the same manner as conventional sectional track. Most brands provide mounting holes, although some require holes to be drilled through with a pin vise and small bit, **29**.

Always wear eye protection when laying track—small nails and spikes can shoot out of pliers with amazing speed.

Adhesive

You can also glue track in place. This is a good alternative when the roadbed is laid directly on extruded foam, as the foam will not hold nails and spikes securely. It also works well on wood subroadbed. If you do this, think of it as permanent—it's difficult to salvage track once it has been glued in place.

Latex construction adhesive, such as Liquid Nails for Projects, works well for this. It's available in tubes that fit into a caulking gun and also in smaller squeeze-style tubes. Buy the type designed for foam or craft projects.

Work in small areas—a piece or two of track at a time. Run a bead of adhesive down the middle of the roadbed. With a putty knife, smooth the adhesive into a thin layer, **30**. It doesn't take much adhesive to hold the track firmly, and you don't want excess glue oozing up between the ties.

Press the track firmly into place, making sure that all track joints are aligned properly and that both rail joiners are securely in place, **31**. You can use push pins or weights to hold the track in place if necessary until the glue dries. Don't place adhesive near turnout throw bars or point rails, **32**. A bit of adhesive under the end ties of each turnout will be more than enough to keep them in place.

Adhesive also works for securing all-in-one track, **33**. Spread a thin layer of adhesive on the surface and then press the track in place, **34**. You may need to place weights atop the track to keep it in firm contact with the layout surface while the glue dries, **35**.

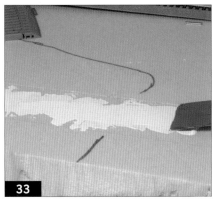

33

I applied a layer of Woodland Scenics Foam Tack Glue on top of this foam layout table, then spread it evenly with a putty knife.

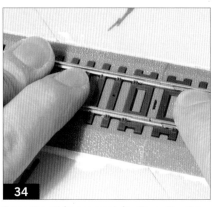

34

Press the all-in-one track in place atop the adhesive—in this case, HO scale Atlas True-Track. Make sure the sections are aligned.

35

Weights (assorted bottles and soda cans work well) will hold the track in place until the adhesive dries.

36

To provide room for rail joiners used with flextrack, trim off the end tie with a hobby knife.

37

Spike the flextrack in place but leave an inch or two straight at the end and trim the ends so they're even.

38

Make sure the joint between flextrack pieces is square and then solder both rail joiners in place.

Cleaning track

Track gets dirty over time. Part of this is oxidation, a film that forms on the rail because of contact with the air. Track also collects dust and dirt that's always present and floating around.

The most popular way to clean track, especially on a small layout, is with an abrasive track cleaner. Several companies make them; they look like a large ink eraser. Rubbing it along the rail removes grime and oxidation. Be careful around turnouts; too much pressure on points can bend or break them. After track cleaning, use a small handheld vacuum to remove debris.

Rubbing an abrasive track cleaner along a rail will remove rust, dirt, and oxidation.

Flextrack

To lay flextrack, follow the same steps as with sectional track. Flextrack gets a bit trickier in curves, but it's not difficult to cut and fit with some practice and the proper methods (see the sidebar on page 41 for hints on cutting track). You'll need to trim away a tie at the end of the flextrack to clear space for rail joiners, **36**. Make sure the rail ends are even to match with the adjoining track section.

For flextrack joints on curves, start by forming the flextrack to the proper shape. If the free end is to be straight, trim the rail ends even, double-check the original track joint, and secure the piece.

If the free end will continue a curve with another section, spike or nail the first piece in place, but leave an inch or two of the free end straight and trim the rail ends even, **37**. Bend the next section to the proper radius,

39

Continue laying the track through the joint, treating it as a single long piece of flextrack.

40

Clean up the top and inside of each rail with a needle file to ensure smooth operation through the joint.

41

The three wood ties in the middle blend in with the other ties. All have been painted various shades of flat brown.

42

Floquil's weathering markers make it easy to paint the sides of rails, which eliminates the unrealistic shine.

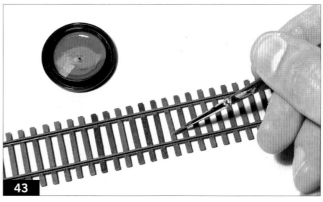

43

Put a few drops of various brown and rust colors in an old plastic lid and use a brush to paint the rail or individual ties.

also leaving about an inch of the end straight, and match it with the first section. Join the sections with rail joiners and solder each joint, **38**. Hold the iron to the rail joiner and both rails and then touch the solder to the joint on each side of the iron until the solder flows into the joiner (see Chapter 7 for more tips on soldering).

With the pieces soldered together, work with it as a single long piece, bending it to the needed radius. This eliminates the potential for kinks at the joint and results in a smooth, flowing curve, **39**. Use a needle file to clean the joint, making sure that the top and inside of the railhead are smooth, **40**.

As you lay flextrack—on curves as well as straight sections—make sure the track stays in alignment. One way is to hold a steel straightedge along an outside rail, but I've found the best way is to simply get down to track level and sight along the rails. You will quickly spot any

places where the track jogs out of alignment.

Slip ties under the rails where there are gaps. These can be the ties you cut away from the flextrack (with the spike detail removed to clear) or low-profile wood ties stained or painted to match adjoining ties, **41**. Glue them in place with cyanoacrylate adhesive.

Leave small gaps (no more than ¹⁄₁₆") in rail joints every three or four feet to allow for expansion and contraction of layout materials. Many modelers solder all other rail joints to ensure good electrical contact, but I would consider this an optional step, especially on a small layout.

Painting track

One problem with model track is that the rails are bright and shiny. Although the tops of prototype rails are shiny, the sides are various shades of rust. Among the easiest and fastest ways of painting model track is with Floquil's line of weathering markers,

which dispense paint via felt-tip applicators, **42**. The set includes three rust colors that can be varied. Simply run the markers along the rail sides to coat them. If any paint gets on the tops of the rails, remove it with an abrasive track cleaning block.

A small brush and conventional paint also work well but will take a bit longer. Rail brown, railroad tie brown, roof brown, or any other flat brown paint will suffice. You can also paint the ties as well (which will help get rid of their plastic shine), using various shades of brown, gray, and black. Vary the appearance of each tie for a realistic effect, **43**.

All that's left is to ballast the track. Some modelers prefer ballasting before the scenery is in place; I recommend doing it afterward for the best appearance. Ballasting looks difficult, but it's actually quite easy to do, and it's the final step in making your trackwork realistic. Turn to Chapter 9 to see how to do it.

CHAPTER SEVEN

Wiring a layout

Wiring a layout may seem like an intimidating task, but it is actually a relatively simple process when you use the correct components.

Getting one train moving is a relatively simple feat. However, most modelers eventually want to run two or more trains at the same time. In the past, this has meant complex wiring with toggle switches and electrical blocks, 1; today, Digital Command Control (DCC) makes it easier.

DC track circuit

Direction of travel

Motor

Polarity

−

+

Motor

Polarity

+

Direction of travel

2

3

This Tech 4 from Model Rectifier is an example of a high-quality power pack. Along with speed and direction, it offers momentum and brake controls.

Basics of electricity

You don't have to be an electrical engineer to get a model railroad up and running, but a basic knowledge of electricity will certainly help you both in operating trains and powering electrically powered accessories such as streetlights, structure lights, and switch machines.

Electricity is measured in volts (V) and amperes (A). The voltage represents the force of electricity available on a circuit. Amperes is the amount of power used by any given accessory. As an example, let's look at a typical 110V household circuit. All lights, appliances, and electronic items that you plug into a wall socket run on that 110 volts, but each draws a varying amount of current (amperage).

For example, a clock-radio doesn't require much power to operate. It has a small transformer that continually draws about .1A. A space heater, on the other hand, requires much more power and might draw 10 amps.

Electricity is either alternating current (AC) or direct current (DC). With alternating current, electrons rapidly change directions (alternate) back and forth (120 times per second in the 60-cycle—or 60-hertz—standard of U.S. electrical systems). Toy trains (such as O gauge and American Flyer S gauge) run on AC, and many accessories also use AC.

Most scale model trains (an exception is Märklin HO) operate on DC.

4

Output terminals on this MRC Tech II power pack include variable DC (track power) as well as fixed AC and fixed DC voltage to power accessories.

With direct current, electrons flow in one direction: from the negative pole to the positive pole, **2**. The positive and negative qualities constitute the polarity—a wire, terminal, or rail has a positive or negative polarity. Reversing engine direction is a matter of reversing the current flow, usually via a slide switch on the power pack.

For a locomotive or accessory to work, electricity must flow through a complete circuit. Interrupting the circuit intentionally (such as with an on/off switch) or accidentally (such as a loose rail joiner or broken wire) will shut off any electrical devices on that circuit.

A short circuit is caused when a circuit is completed without passing through a motor, light, or other device that provides resistance. For example,

if a metal screwdriver is accidentally placed across the rails, the electricity takes that path (the short path, or short circuit) instead of going through the locomotive motor. Because there's almost no resistance to the flow of energy, the power supply puts out all of its power at once. This creates an overload that can damage the power supply and other components.

Household circuits in the United States operate at 110 volts AC, but model railroads require much less energy to run. Most model circuits operate from 12V to 16V. Because current draws are also lower, we often measure amperage in milliamps (mA), and each milliamp is ¹⁄₁₀₀₀ of an amp. Thus, 100 mA is .1A; 500 mA is .5A, and so on.

Insulated track section for storing a locomotive or train

Insulated joiner

Insulated joiner

SPST
toggle switch

Power pack

5

Cab control with common-rail wiring

Block 1

Block 2

Common rail

Block 5

Block 3

Block 4

1 2 3 4 5

A B   A B   A B   A B   A B

SPDT
Switches

Common connection

Cab A

Cab B

6

Power packs and transformers

There are several ways to control trains. Until the coming of Digital Command Control, the standard method was using a DC power pack, which has a controller that allows an operator to vary the voltage to the tracks. This method is known as standard DC control.

You'll sometimes hear the terms *transformer* and *power pack* used interchangeably, but there is a significant difference. In train-control terms, a transformer is a controller that steps down household voltage but has an AC output. These are designed for use with toy trains.

A power pack includes a transformer (to step down household voltage to the 12-16V needed for model locomotives) but also has a bridge rectifier (a series of four diodes) that converts the transformer's AC output to the DC required for scale trains.

Power packs are rated by their power output. Some small packs, especially those included in basic train sets, are rated below 1A, which is enough to power a single locomotive. Even adding a second locomotive can drop the power considerably. More robust packs with ratings from 1A to 2A are available from MRC and several other companies.

Basic power packs have a speed control knob and a direction control switch. Some higher-quality packs have additional features, **3**. These include momentum control and braking, where the throttle settings gradually change to mimic the gradual acceleration and deceleration of real trains.

Some power packs have built-in circuit breakers that protect the unit in case of a short circuit. Others have indicator lights for power and short circuits, and some have a built-in voltmeter and/or ammeter.

Most packs have two sets of output terminals: one set that goes to the track (labeled "track" or "variable DC") and a second set, usually AC, designed to power accessories (labeled "accessories" or "fixed AC" and often labeled with the output voltage), **4**. The accessory output can be used to power items such as streetlights, structure lights, and switch machines.

Most power packs are designed to rest on a shelf or flat base. The operator must stand or sit by the pack to operate the controls. Walkaround power packs offer tethered or wireless handheld throttles. These allow an operator to move to follow a train, which is handy on medium- and large-size layouts.

If you have a small layout and plan to be the only operator, a single power pack is all you need. You don't have to worry about dividing your layout into blocks for multiple-train control.

You will, however, eventually want to have more than one locomotive on your layout or want to store a train on a siding or spur track. You can do this by adding a simple on/off switch—such as a single-pole, single-throw (SPST) toggle—to control a section of track, **5**. You'll need to electrically isolate the section with gaps in one rail as the drawing shows.

Most modelers eventually want to run two or more trains at once—letting one train run on a main line while switching on a branch or having another operator so both can simultaneously control their trains. We'll look at a couple of ways of accomplishing this, including traditional cab control and command control.

Digital Command Control (DCC) basic system

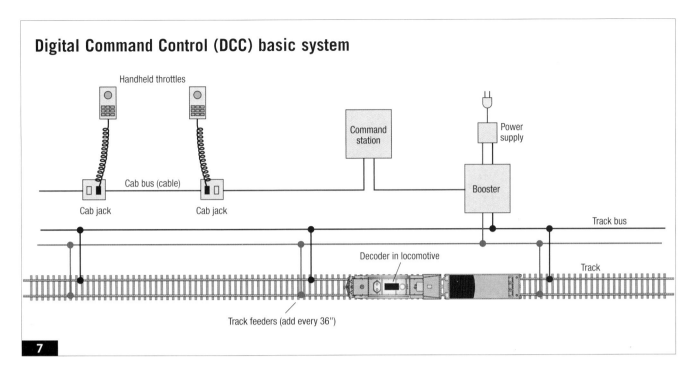

Handheld throttles

Cab bus (cable)

Cab jack   Cab jack

Command station

Power supply

Booster

Track bus

Decoder in locomotive

Track

Track feeders (add every 36")

7

Traditional cab control

Although DCC has become the system of choice for most serious model railroaders, conventional DC block or cab control is still a viable option. This is especially true for small layouts where only one or two operators are likely to be running trains at one time.

The basic idea is to divide the track into electrically isolated sections called blocks. Each block has a single-pole, double-throw (SPDT), center-off toggle switch that shifts control for that block to either of two power packs, **6**, or simply turns the block off. The drawing shows common-rail wiring, where one rail carries the return power for both cabs.

There are few rules in dividing your layout into blocks, but blocks should be at least as long as your average train length, each siding should be its own block, and each yard track should be its own block.

Blocks must be insulated from each other. The easiest way to do this is using plastic insulated rail joiners at the block boundaries (see Chapter 6) when you initially build a layout. If the layout is already built, you can cut gaps in rails with a cutoff disk in a motor tool (be sure to wear eye protection) or with a razor saw, which is a slower process. If you do this, glue a small piece of plastic in the gap to keep the rail ends from touching.

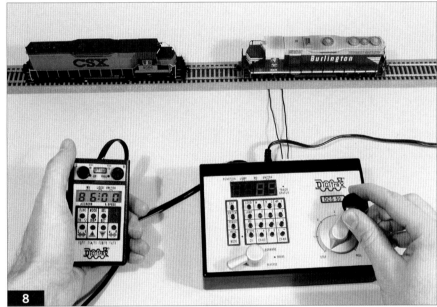

8 The Digitrax Zephyr is a basic DCC system. The box combines the command station, booster, and a stationary throttle. Additional handheld cabs can also be plugged in.

The wiring itself is rather simple, but there can be a lot of it. Run one control wire from each power pack to the terminal on the opposite side of each toggle switch. This way, the control of each block will be indicated by the direction the toggle switch is pointing. Do the same for the second power pack.

Run the wire from the center pole of each toggle switch to the rail of the appropriate block. Color-coding the wire helps keep track of things: for example,

make the common rail wire blue, the control wire from power pack A yellow, the control wire from power pack B green, and wires to the blocks red.

Digital Command Control

Few technological developments have impacted model railroading the way that the emergence of command control revolutionized wiring and operating trains. No longer are toggle or rotary switches needed to assign blocks to power packs.

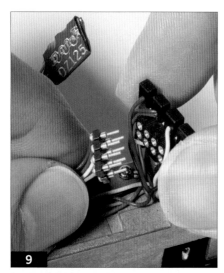

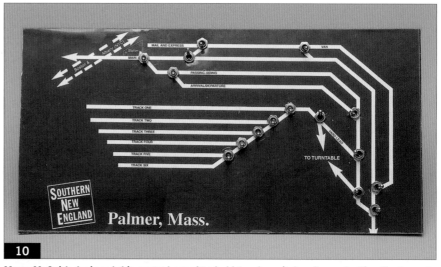

9 Some model locomotives have sockets that enable modelers to easily add plug-equipped DCC decoders.

10 Marty McGuirk designed this control panel to hold toggle switches for controlling the turnouts on his layout. Panels can also hold block-power-control toggle switches. He designed the panel on a computer and printed it out. *Marty McGuirk*

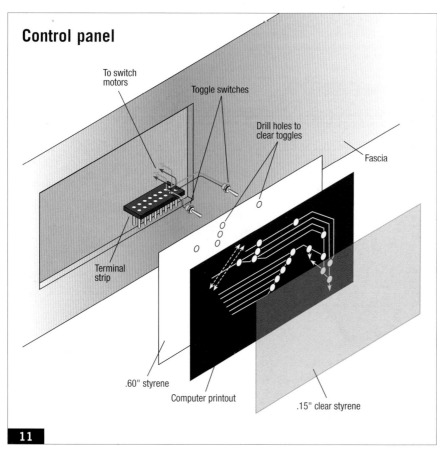

Control panel

To switch motors

Toggle switches

Drill holes to clear toggles

Fascia

Terminal strip

.60" styrene

Computer printout

.15" clear styrene

11 Marty mounted his control panel vertically on the fascia of his layout as shown.

With command control, a controller sends a signal and power through the rails, and devices (receivers or decoders) in each locomotive decipher the signals and respond only to those sent by a particular throttle. This allows two or more operators to control their trains independently of each other on the same track.

Command control systems have been available since the 1960s, but early systems presented significant challenges. Systems were expensive, receivers were bulky, a lot of wiring work was required, and operation wasn't always reliable. Even as cost came down and reliability increased through the 1980s,

a big problem remained because command control systems were proprietary: each manufacturer used a different protocol (method of communication among throttles, command stations, and receivers), and none were compatible with each other. This locked a buyer into a complete system. If a company went out of business, its users were simply out of luck.

DCC emerged as a standard protocol adopted by manufacturers with the guidance of the National Model Railroad Association in the 1990s. The common protocol allows users of any system to operate locomotives with decoders made by any number of manufacturers. The digital basis allows software and other features to continually develop.

Current DCC system manufacturers include CVP Products (Easy DCC), Digitrax, Lenz, MRC (Model Rectifier Corp.), NCE (North Coast Engineering), PSI (Power Systems Inc.), and others. Additional companies specialize in sound decoders (such as QSI and Soundtraxx) or additional DCC accessories.

The basics of how DCC works are shown in photo **7**. One or more handheld cabs, also called throttles (which can be tethered or wireless), send signals to the command station. The command station compiles these signals and sends data to a booster, which provides the power and sends both the

Types of reversing tracks

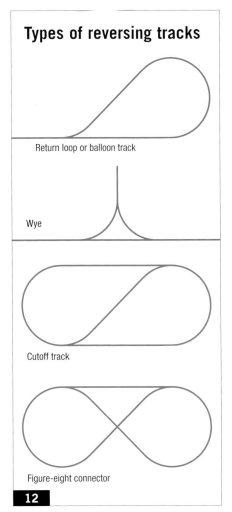

Return loop or balloon track

Wye

Cutoff track

Figure-eight connector

12

Reversing tracks require special wiring to avoid short circuits. These are the most common types of reverse loops.

Loop short circuits

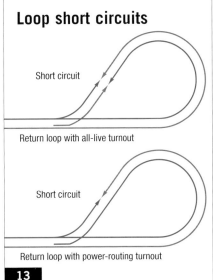

Short circuit

Return loop with all-live turnout

Short circuit

Return loop with power-routing turnout

13

Two-switch method

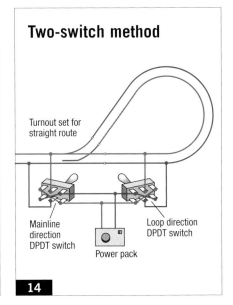

Turnout set for straight route

Mainline direction DPDT switch

Power pack

Loop direction DPDT switch

14

Wiring live-frog turnouts

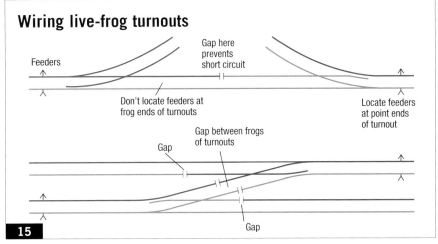

Feeders

Gap here prevents short circuit

Don't locate feeders at frog ends of turnouts

Locate feeders at point ends of turnout

Gap between frogs of turnouts

Gap

Gap

15

command signals and control power to the track via the track bus. Decoders on each locomotive interpret the DCC signal, with each decoder responding only to those commands coming from the selected throttle.

Most DCC manufacturers offer basic or starter systems, **8**. Some, such as the Digitrax Zephyr system pictured, have the command station and booster combined in a single box; some also include a stationary throttle on the command station.

Installation on a small layout is relatively simple. In theory, you only need to connect the two wires from your DCC booster to the layout. However, to ensure a good signal and ample power throughout the layout, it's a good idea to add multiple track feeders—a set of feeders about every 36" of track will suffice.

In the early days of DCC, wiring and soldering was required to install decoders in their locomotives. That's not really the case anymore since many locomotives are available today with the option of a factory-installed decoder—many of which include sound (see photo 12 in Chapter 10). This is definitely the way to go for a first layout.

Many other locomotives can be converted to DCC relatively easily, either by plugging a decoder into a socket on the model's circuit board, **9**, or by replacing the model's circuit board with a circuit-board-type decoder. Most hobby shops that deal in DCC products will be happy to help you match a decoder to a locomotive; most DCC manufacturers also have websites that are very helpful in this regard.

Parallel and series circuits

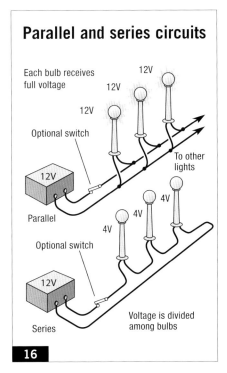

Each bulb receives full voltage

12V

12V

12V

12V

Optional switch

12V

To other lights

Parallel

4V

4V

4V

Optional switch

12V

Series

Voltage is divided among bulbs

16

Hold the iron against the rail and wire, and touch the solder to both. Remove the iron when the solder starts to flow.

Insulation-displacement connectors (IDCs) allow you to connect wires without soldering. The main wire passes through the IDC, with the smaller wire stub-ending. Squeezing the metal piece makes the connection through the insulation.

DCC is expandable, so the same system you buy for your first layout can be used for a later, larger layout. DCC offers tremendous versatility in operation, even for small layouts. If possible, visit a DCC-powered layout to see what it can offer for you.

Wiring for DCC becomes more complex on larger layouts. See a book such as *Basic DCC Wiring for Your Model Railroad* by Mike Polsgrove (Kalmbach Books, 2011) for more details on DCC systems, wiring, and decoder installation.

Control panel

You might need a control panel to hold block-control or switch-machine toggle switches, **10**. The traditional method is to add a track diagram to tempered hardboard (such as Masonite) or thin plywood.

To make a painted diagram, start by painting the board white. Use thin masking tape or pinstriping tape to mark the track diagram onto the board. Indicate block boundaries by cutting gaps in the tape at these locations. Spray-paint the board black or another contrasting color. When the paint dries, peel off the tape to reveal the white track diagram. Add decal or dry-transfer lettering as needed.

A method that has become much more popular recently is drawing the plan on a computer with graphics software and printing it out. This makes it easier to include lettering and graphics.

A thin sheet of clear styrene or acrylic over the plan will protect it, **11**. With either method, drill holes at appropriate locations to mount toggle switches.

The panel can be mounted to the layout in a number of ways, including vertically on the edge of the layout, on the fascia, or on a table or shelf in front of the layout.

Reverse-loop and wye wiring

Reverse loops tend to cause more headaches for beginners than any other wiring issue. Regardless of whether you have DCC, cab control, or just a single block of track, you need to employ special wiring if your layout has a reverse loop or reversing tracks, **12**. These include any loop of track that enables a train to double back on itself or a wye that allows a train or locomotive to turn—basically, any time a train can start in one direction and end up back at that spot pointed in the opposite direction.

The reason is track polarity, **13**. As the drawings show, the positive rail will eventually bump into the negative, resulting in a short circuit. The solution is to gap the rails entering and leaving the loop, making the loop a separate electrical block. If you're using a single power pack or cab control, the best way of controlling it is to wire the loop track with two double-pole, double-throw (DPDT) toggle switches, **14**. The loop direction switch is thrown before the train

enters the loop. Once the train is in the loop, the mainline direction switch is thrown, allowing the train to continue running as it exits the loop back to the main line. A wye can be wired in the same manner, designating one leg of the wye as the loop track.

Special turnout wiring

The type of turnouts you install will affect how you wire your layout. All commercial turnouts are one of two types: all-live or power-routing. To keep wiring simple, many beginners opt to stick with all-live turnouts.

On an all-live turnout, both legs of the turnout are always live, with the proper polarity routed to each rail. This is done by isolating the frog (the point where the rails meet) and making it electrically dead. This avoids the short circuit that would result from the meeting of two live rails of opposite polarity. Internal jumpers route power around the frog and provide power to the points.

No special wiring is required for all-live turnouts. Most sectional track turnouts fit this category including Atlas, Bachmann EZ Track, Life-Like Power-Loc, Kato Unitrack, Micro Engineering, Peco's Insulfrog line, and the current line of Walthers HO turnouts (made by Shinohara) labeled as "DCC friendly."

With a power-routing turnout, the frog is live. This means that only the

Soldering

Whether you're dealing with track power or accessories, it's vital that your electrical connections be solid. Problems such as short circuits, broken wires, and intermittent connections are frustrating and can be hard to trace and difficult to correct. The best way to avoid problems is to do it right the first time.

Soldering is a basic skill that will come in handy in many areas of the hobby. You'll need a medium-power (30 watts or so) pencil-type soldering iron. A larger soldering gun will also work, but you'll find it cumbersome for many hobby projects.

A pointed or chisel-shaped tip works best. Use a fine metal file to shape the tip and to remove any corrosion or oxidation. The tip must be tinned to work properly. To tin the tip, plug in the iron or turn it on until it is hot. Touch solder to the tip and make sure it coats the filed surface. Keep a damp sponge handy and quickly wipe the tinned tip across the sponge. You are now ready to solder.

For electrical work, use resin-core solder. A 60/40 tin/lead solder works well; resin-core, lead-free solders are also available. Never use acid-core solder, as electricity will eventually cause the acid to corrode the joint.

Wrap wires securely when joining them. You can use a knife to remove the insulation, but I highly recommend a wire stripper—they work quickly and won't damage the wire. For a tee joint, wrap the butt-end wire tightly around the main wire a few times. For end-to-end joints, wrap each end around the other.

Place the iron firmly against the joint, making sure the iron contacts both wires. As the joint becomes hot, touch the solder against both wires on the side opposite the iron (not against the iron). This ensures that the solder will flow freely into the joint itself, and not merely melt against the iron and stick loosely to the wires. Remove the iron and let the joint cool for a few seconds without moving.

The solder should appear shiny and should cover both wires. If the wires move as the solder cools, the joint will be weak—often apparent by the solder having a crystallized, dull look. Fix this by reheating the joint with the iron until the solder flows again.

I keep a damp paper towel handy to press against the joint to speed the cooling process. Avoid breathing the smoke and fumes while soldering and be sure to wear eye protection to protect yourself from any stray solder that spatters.

Hold the iron to both wires. Touch the solder to the joint until it flows freely on both wires.

A soldering iron stand holds the iron securely. The damp sponge helps keep the tip of the iron clean.

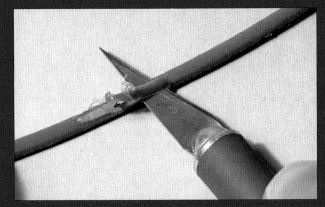

A hobby knife will strip insulation from wire. Be careful not to cut or nick the wire itself, which can weaken it.

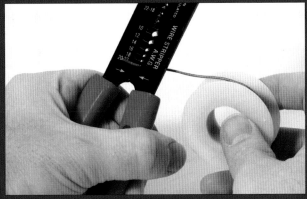

A wire stripper is the best and fastest way to remove insulation from stranded or solid wire.

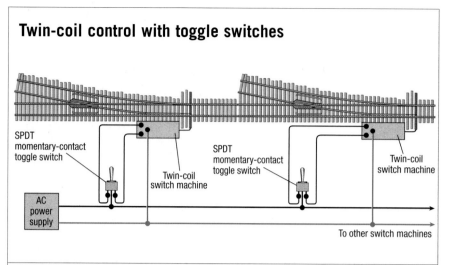

Twin-coil control with toggle switches

SPDT momentary-contact toggle switch

Twin-coil switch machine

SPDT momentary-contact toggle switch

Twin-coil switch machine

AC power supply

To other switch machines

Twin-coil control with Atlas-style control boxes

Twin-coil switch machine

Twin-coil switch machine

AC power supply

To other controllers

19

trains, but—especially with a train-set power pack—that can limit the power available to run trains. It's best to have a separate power supply. If you've upgraded from a train-set power pack to a nicer one for running trains, this is a great application for using the train-set pack.

With lights, it's always best to operate them at a lower voltage than their rating—for example, run 14V bulbs at 12V. This will tone down the effect a bit and make the bulbs last much longer than when powering them at full voltage.

Track feeders

When starting with a simple oval of track, connecting two wires to the rails is usually enough. With more complex track plans, you'll find you need additional track feeders. Rail has some resistance to it, meaning the voltage drops the farther a train is from the feeder locations. Rail joints can also add to that problem, as rail joiners don't always conduct electricity well. Cab control helps combat voltage drops because each block has its own feeders and is relatively short.

I suggest adding track feeders every three or four feet of track. If you use cab control, you'll need at least one set of feeders for every isolated block section.

You can employ a couple of methods to get power to the rails. The handiest—provided you know where you want them when you lay track—is using rail joiners with feeder wires attached to them (see Chapter 6).

Soldering feeders directly to the rails works well (see the sidebar on page 55 for tips on soldering). Drill a hole through the roadbed and table next to the rail where you want to add the feeder (a rail joint is a good spot). Strip insulation from the end of a wire and bend it to a right angle, so it is wedged to the side of the rail.

Place the hot soldering iron so it contacts both the rail and wire, **17**. Touch the solder to the joint away from the iron—you want the heat from the parts, not the iron, to melt the solder. When the solder starts to flow, remove the iron.

route selected by the points is powered with the proper polarity, **15**. Special wiring is needed because if two of these turnouts are placed frog to frog, a short circuit will result. You need to provide gaps between frogs and make sure track feeders supply power from the point end (not the frog end) of these turnouts.

Examples of power-routing turnouts include Peco ElectroFrog HO and N scale turnouts and older Walthers HO turnouts (made by Shinohara).

Accessory wiring

If you have accessories on your layout, you'll need to supply power to them and control them. The most common accessories are streetlights, internal structure lights, and other lights.

These can all be placed on the same circuit, provided that you want them all to come on and go off at the same time. Lights can be wired in two ways: in series or in parallel, **16**. Wiring them in series (daisy-chained end to end) is usually not the best option. Each lamp gets a proportional share of the voltage. In other words, on a 12-volt circuit with three lamps each lamp would get 4 volts.

Wiring them in parallel is a better choice. Each gets the full voltage from the circuit; if one lamp burns out, it won't affect the others; and it's reasonably simple to add additional lamps if needed. A SPST toggle switch easily controls the lamps.

The keys to wiring these items are that all accessories on a circuit be rated for the same voltage and that the total current draw of all accessories does not exceed that of your power supply.

Many beginners simply connect this circuit to the "accessories" terminal of the power pack used for running

If you're using DC cab control, you can run no. 20 wire directly from the toggle switch to the track. If your layout is wired as a single block, I'd suggest running a track bus of heavier wire (no. 16 or 18), with no. 20 or 22 track feeders dropping down to the bus. For DCC, use a track bus of no. 14 or 16 wire, with no. 20 or 22 track feeders. I prefer solid (not stranded) wire for most wiring.

You can solder connections or you can use insulation-displacement connectors (IDCs), also called suitcase connectors, **18**. Available in several sizes, IDCs have a metal connector that cuts through the insulation to make a connection. They are quick and easy to use.

Run wires in an orderly manner under your benchwork. A wide variety of wire ties, clips, and hangers are available for bundling wiring. This makes it much easier to troubleshoot any problems that develop. Also, label everything—don't rely on your memory. I simply write the information on the benchwork itself.

Switch machines

If you choose to power your turnouts, you have a couple of choices to make. You can buy powered turnouts or you can buy manual turnouts and add switch machines. If you buy switch machines, you need to choose which type to install.

There are two main types of electric switch machines: twin-coil and slow-motion motor. Twin-coil machines have solenoids that are momentarily energized by a brief burst of electricity. They snap turnout points into position quickly. This is the type that comes mounted on remote-control turnouts. Separate below-table twin-coil machines are available from Atlas, NJ International, Rix, and others.

Slow-motion machines (such as the Circuitron Tortoise and others) rely on a slow-speed, low-current-draw motor to move the points. With these switch machines, the power is always on. The motor stalls in the direction the turnout is thrown, but its design allows it to do so without damage.

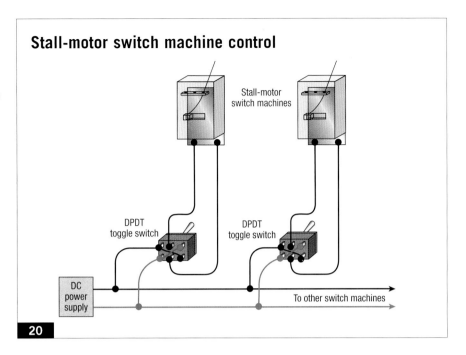

Stall-motor switch machine control

Stall-motor switch machines

DPDT toggle switch

DPDT toggle switch

DC power supply

To other switch machines

20

Many beginners simply choose remote-control turnouts with twin-coil machines mounted on the side. These are relatively inexpensive, most include the control switch, and they're easy to install and wire. Their main disadvantage is appearance: the switch machines look rather bulky and are quite unrealistic.

The best solution for appearance is to buy manual turnouts and power them with switch machines mounted under the table (see photo 14 in Chapter 6). This takes more work, but you'll certainly appreciate the appearance when you're done. You don't have to do this when you build your layout. If in doubt, drill access holes for the control rod when laying your track even if your initial plans don't involve powered turnouts. You'll appreciate this effort if you choose to add under-table switch machines later.

Mounting under-table machines involves threading the control wire through the access hole into a hole drilled in the throw bar. The machine must be screwed into place under the table—most manufacturers include a drilling template to make this easier.

Wiring is different for twin-coil and slow-motion machines. For twin-coil machines on small layouts, a 14 to 18-volt AC power supply will work, **19**. Here's a good use for a train-set power pack. Although you can use the accessory terminals on the same pack you use for train control, I don't recommend it, as your trains can slow down noticeably every time a turnout is thrown (especially if multiple turnouts are thrown at once).

Momentary-contact switches are needed. If power is applied to a turnout for more than a second or two, the solenoid can burn out. You can use the Atlas-style control buttons that most manufacturers supply with their remote turnouts. The drawing also shows how to use single-pole, double-throw, momentary-contact toggle switches (which are more easily tied to a track diagram on a control panel). The key is that these toggles must be the momentary-contact type, in which the toggle is spring-loaded and returns itself to the center-off position.

One method of wiring slow-motion machines is shown in figure **20**, using a 12-volt DC power supply with DPDT toggle switches controlling the machines.

Most slow-motion machines (and some twin-coil versions) include an extra set or two of electrical contacts. These can be used to route power to the turnout frog with power-routing turnouts, or they can control lineside signals or indicator lights on a control panel. For details, see Andy Sperandeo's excellent book *Easy Model Railroad Wiring* (Kalmbach Books).

1

CHAPTER EIGHT

Modeling structures

A row of storefront structures helps make this HO city scene look realistic.

Structures are vital to making model trains look like they fit into the real world. Kits and fully assembled buildings are available to represent many types of prototype structures. Buildings can help place a layout in a time and place, and with added details, they can serve as the centerpiece of many scenes, 1.

2

Woodland Scenics has HO structures in assembled, detailed, and weathered versions, including Clyde & Dale's Barrel Factory. The crossing tower and sheds are prebuilt structures from Walthers.

3

This Walthers HO building is typical of simple plastic kits. It includes multicolor castings, separate windows, and press-fit joints.

Types of structure models

Thousands of structure kits and assembled buildings are available from many manufacturers across all scales. They include houses, storefronts, and factories along with depots, interlocking towers, and other railroad buildings. You'll find kits for many other related items such as bridges, water towers, and coaling stations.

Many nice buildings are available fully assembled and ready to place on a layout—some are even painted, detailed, and weathered, **2**. By and large, however, structures come as kits requiring at least some assembly.

Structure kits fall into several categories. The most popular are injection-molded styrene kits. These have walls molded with brick, clapboard, or another surface texture. Some have all or most details molded in place, while others have separate window frames and details.

Complexity ranges from very simple assembly (joining four walls together and adding a roof) to intricate (having multiple wall panels, separate windows and doors, and multipart roofs with separate details). Most plastic kits are reasonably easy to assemble. The more-complex ones can be time consuming, but they aren't difficult if you take them step by step.

Basic plastic kit construction

Let's go through the steps of assembling a basic plastic structure kit. The Walthers HO scale River Road Mercantile is relatively simple to build, and the contents

4

Sprue nippers make quick work of removing parts from their casting lugs.

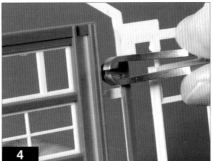

5

Injection-molded parts are usually numbered on the part itself or on the neighboring sprue.

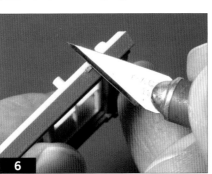

6

A hobby knife will take care of cleaning up sprue cuts or molding flash.

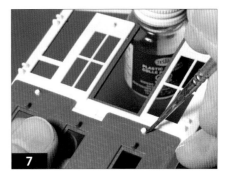

7

Dip a brush in liquid plastic cement and touch it to the joint or mounting peg. Capillary action pulls the glue into the joint.

of the box are shown in photo **3**. During the process, follow the kit's directions as you go, but read ahead a few steps to make sure that something you do early in the process doesn't hinder a later step.

Start by removing parts from their sprues, **4**. For small kits, you can do this all at once; for larger kits, remove the parts as you need them, especially if the sprue is labeled with the part numbers, **5**. This will avoid confusion with

similar-looking parts. Clean up any molding flash or nubs left from cutting parts from sprues, **6**.

The mercantile kit has pegs that align pieces at most joints and help secure them. Put the parts together and add liquid plastic cement with a brush to allow capillary action to pull glue into the joint, **7**. Always add glue from behind a wall and other joints to minimize the risk of glue seeping onto visible surfaces. For

8 For flat surfaces, apply gel-style cement with the bottle's needle-tip applicator and then press the piece in place.

9 Some structures include bases. You can glue the walls to the base as you assemble the structure, which will keep parts aligned.

10 Signs include Microscale decals (bottom left) and paper signs from JL Innovative Design, Blair Line, and City Classics.

11 Cut out the sign with a hobby knife. Use a straightedge as a guide to ensure that the edges will be straight and square.

12 Add cyanoacrylate adhesive with a toothpick and place the sign with tweezers.

13 Signs give a finished structure a lived-in look and indicate its purpose on a layout.

14 Clamp walls together and then apply liquid plastic cement from the rear of the joint.

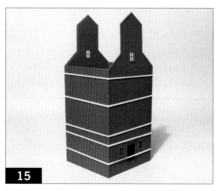

15 Rubber bands can be handy for holding larger structures together when gluing.

joining parts with large surface areas, apply gel-type plastic cement to one surface, **8**, and then press the parts together.

For easiest access, it's generally a good idea to apply windows and other wall details before putting the walls together. Some structures include bases, and using them is a matter of choice. This building includes a front sidewalk and rear sidewalk that also serves as a stairway base, so I used it, **9**. I painted the base a concrete color before adding the structure walls. You can also skip the base and install the structure directly on your layout.

I didn't glue the roof in place on the building—this allows easier access in case I decide to add interior details or lighting in the future. I did, however, paint the roof grimy black. (See Chapter 12 for tips on painting.)

I also added signs to the building, but I chose not to use the ones included with the kit. Many companies offer signs that can be used on structures of all scales, including Bar Mills, Blair Line, and JL Innovative Design. Most of these are printed on heavy paper, **10**. Microscale has a number of decal sign and lettering sets, and Clover House and Woodland Scenics have dry-transfer (rub-on) lettering and signs.

Look for other sources of signs as well. Almost any item that includes a company name, logo, or herald can be used, including stationery, envelopes, business cards, packaging, and old road maps (for oil companies). You can also take photos of real signs or find graphics online and print them out for your own use. Just remember that you cannot legally copy and distribute trademarked or copyrighted materials.

The main structure sign is from a Blair Line set. Cut it out with a small sharp scissors or a hobby knife, **11**. Apply a bit of cyanoacrylate adhesive (CA) to the building at the sign location with a toothpick and carefully set the sign in place, **12**. I added several additional product posters and signs to the side of the building, trying to give it a look of a rural or small-time grocery store in the late steam era, **13**.

Often the biggest challenge in building plastic structures is gluing walls together. Generally, the best method is gluing one joint at a time, **14**. If the joint fits well, you can often hold the pieces in place by hand until the glue begins to set. Small bar clamps can also be used to hold the walls together. For large or tall structures, placing rubber bands around the entire building also works, **15**. Once the walls are in place, use a brush to apply liquid plastic cement from inside each corner.

Wood kits

Most wood kits on the market today feature laser-cut basswood components and represent wood prototypes with clapboard or board-and-batten siding, **16**. Walls, roof sections, and other large pieces often have tabs and slots to make construction and alignment easy. Even small trim pieces are laser-cut to size, **17**. These kits are more difficult to assemble than an average plastic kit because the parts are more delicate, and the components must be painted before or during assembly. However, they are not out of reach of a beginning modeler who has assembled a plastic kit or two. Here are several tips when assembling laser-cut kits:

- Use a hobby knife or single-edge razor blade to finish cutting parts from their sheets.
- Choose yellow glue for securing parts.
- Paint the structure in subassemblies, making sure window parts are painted before adding clear plastic glass.
- Prime both sides of each wall to avoid warping. Household latex interior wood primer works well for the initial coat—I put some in a two-ounce bottle, so it is handy to use.
- Brush-painting works well—follow the wood grain for best results.

Craftsman kits

Another type of wood structure kit is the craftsman kit. Many of these are offered in limited runs by manufacturers. These might have some larger pieces (such as walls) that are precut, but they rely on the modeler to cut dimensional wood strips and other components to size. Some include injection-molded plastic or die-cast metal windows and details; others require the modeler to

16
This HO scale American Model Builders interlocking tower was built from a laser-cut wood kit.

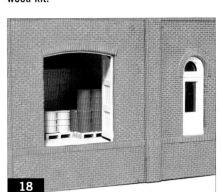

18

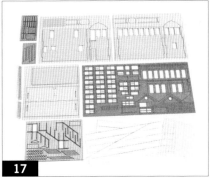

17
Here's how a typical laser-cut kit looks straight from the box. This is another American Model Builders interlocking tower.

To create the illusion of interior detail, glue a few items onto a simple box made from styrene or cardstock. Glue the box behind an open door, where it will be visible to people viewing the scene.

assemble these items from stripwood. The modeler also has to paint or stain the finished structure.

Craftsman kits can be time consuming and difficult to assemble, but they can also be very rewarding to build. Many model railroaders highly value the model-building aspect of the hobby, and for them, craftsman kits bring a great deal of enjoyment.

Other kits

There are also structure kits that feature cast resin, cast plaster, and etched-metal components. These range from simple to complex construction, and most require painting.

Many modelers also scratchbuild structures, meaning they build them from raw materials and individual detail components. Scratchbuilding might sound intimidating, but a basic scratchbuilding project is usually within reach of most modelers who've built a few kits.

Final details

There are any number of details you can add to structures. Items such as crates

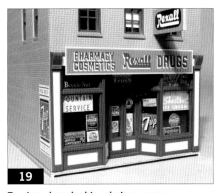

19
To glue signs inside windows, use a toothpick to spread a thin coat of acrylic gloss medium or clear parts cement on the entire face of a sign and then place it in the window. The adhesive will dry clear.

and barrels on a loading dock or inside a door at a factory make buildings appear to be active, **18**.

Some modelers superdetail scenes with buildings that have interior lighting and a high level of interior detail. You can also create the impression of interior detail by gluing signs inside storefront windows, **19**. Window shades can be made by gluing colored cardstock inside the windows.

1

CHAPTER NINE

Adding scenery and details

Yes, this is a model railroad. Lance Mindheim built the scene on his N scale Monon layout, which features late-fall scenery typical of Indiana. Varying scenic levels, the curving waterway, and many textures on the surface all contribute to the scene's realism. *Lance Mindheim*

Nothing turns a collection of trains, track, and structures into a model railroad like scenery, 1. Scenery unifies a layout and makes a scene look real and not just a collection of models on a plywood table. Unfortunately, few areas of the hobby scare as many modelers as scenery. This needn't be the case, as scenery is very forgiving. Basic ground cover and terrain are easy to do, and even detailed scenery can be accomplished by most modelers.

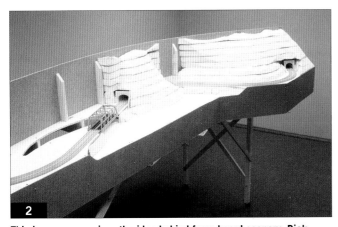

2 This image summarizes the idea behind foam-board scenery. Dick Christiansen applied several layers of foam board to create the scenery profile of his N scale Salt Lake Route layout. *Dick Christiansen*

3 Pelle Søeborg applied pieces of foam on edge over open-grid benchwork on this HO layout. He used a hot-wire tool (foreground) to cut them to shape and then glued them together. *Pelle Søeborg*

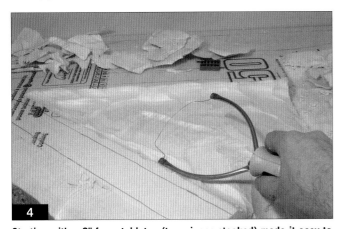

4 Starting with a 3" foam tabletop (two pieces stacked) made it easy to carve below-track features with a hot-wire tool. The wire on this tool from Hot Wire Foam Factory can be bent to various shapes.

5 This layout, built on a foam sheet table, uses Woodland Scenics Foam Inclines (white) along with other pieces of foam to create a scenic terrain. *Jim Kelly*

There's no "best" way to make scenery. There is a tremendous variety of materials available, and the techniques you choose will largely depend on the type of scenery you desire. Are you trying to capture the look of a large, busy city, rolling Midwestern hills, rugged Colorado mountains, or an Arizona desert? We'll hit the highlights of getting a realistic layer of scenery on a layout. For more details, see Dave Frary's *How to Build Realistic Model Railroad Scenery* (Kalmbach Books, 2005).

There are two real parts to scenery construction: making the landform and applying scenic cover and texture. I'll start by reviewing various methods of creating scenic profiles and then show you how to apply ground cover.

Building landforms

The first temptation for most beginners is to simply build everything on a flat tabletop. Although this makes scenery construction easy, it isn't very realistic. Look outside and you'll find that, even on the plains, the ground undulates. There are features above the main ground level—railroads and highways are elevated on roadbed, lawns and ground are terraced, and most areas have at least some hills. There are also plenty of features below ground level, including culverts under roads and railroads, ponds, lakes, rivers, swamps, and valleys.

A giant step toward realism on a model railroad is to include scenic features both above and below track level. Even a couple of details below the surface help eliminate the tabletop appearance.

You should have a good idea of the type of scenery you'll need when designing your track plan since how you build the benchwork top will influence how you add the scenic base. In fact, the benchwork top, trackwork, and scenery processes all naturally flow into each other.

The two most popular methods of forming scenic terrain employ extruded foam board and hardshell plaster. Both have advantages and disadvantages, and you'll find many modelers who swear by each. As you play with various techniques, you might very well find that you like both, and that combining the two methods is often a good approach. Let's look at foam first.

Sheets of extruded polystyrene foam—pink, blue, yellow, or gray, depending upon the manufacturer— gained popularity as a scenic material in the 1970s. This is the foam sold as building and foundation insulation in sheets from ½" to 2" thick, not the white beaded board style of foam.

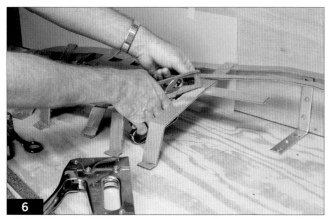

6 Cardboard strips stapled into a web make a good base for hardshell scenery. The backdrop is held in place by a metal L bracket, which will be covered by the scenery. *Jim Kelly*

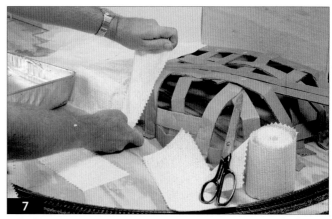

7 Plaster gauze is cut into strips, dipped in water, and draped over the cardboard web. Plaster gauze is available from Woodland Scenics and other manufacturers. *Jim Kelly*

8 Provide level bases for structures with cork, foam, or foam core. The scenery covering can then be applied up to the base.

9 Place a cup or so of Sculptamold in a plastic container and then slowly add water while mixing until the material is saturated.

Sheets of foam can easily be layered atop a benchwork grid or plywood table for various effects: for example, a river bottom on the lowest surface, track level on the next layer up, and hills with the next layers, **2**. It's ideal for level or gently rolling scenery. Foam can also be used to form mountainous areas by either placing it on edge, **3**, or by stacking it in layers and carving it to shape.

Use foam-compatible adhesive, such as Woodland Scenics Foam Tack Glue, when gluing foam pieces together. You might have to add weights to hold pieces in place until the glue sets. With careful carving and shaping, you will need very little additional materials to get a realistic ground surface.

A serrated kitchen knife works well for making initial rough cuts and carving. You can use a rasp, such as a Stanley Surform tool, to shape and contour the rough-cut foam to the final contour. Hot-wire foam tools (avail-

able from Hot Wire Foam Factory and Woodland Scenics) are handy for cutting and shaping foam, **4**. Be sure to use these with adequate ventilation and take care when working with the hot tools to avoid burns.

Another handy foam product is Woodland Scenics line of flexible foam risers and foam inclines, **5**. They are made to go on a tabletop and provide an elevated base for track and roads (like the cookie-cutter method without having to cut the tabletop).

Being extremely lightweight and easy to shape are the biggest advantages of using foam. A downside is that it can take a lot of foam and a lot of carving to get the effects you're looking for, especially on a large layout.

Hardshell scenery

The hardshell scenery method has been around since the early days of the hobby. It involves forming a rough sce-

nic contour with either a web of cardboard strips, **6**, or a web of tape over pieces of wadded-up paper. Cardboard strips can be stapled or hot-glued together, attached to the benchwork, and supported by pieces of wood or foam if necessary.

A layer of plaster-soaked towels or plaster-impregnated gauze is then draped over the scenic form, **7**. Once the plaster hardens, it forms a hard shell—hence the name of the technique. It's a good idea to cover track with masking tape during the process.

The traditional shell method is to mix a batch of plaster, cut paper towels into strips a few inches wide, dip them into the plaster, and place them over the web. Plaster-soaked gauze (available from Woodland Scenics and others) is a bit more expensive, but it is both easier and neater. To use, you cut the pieces of gauze into strips, dip them in water, and apply them to the scenic base.

10 Apply a thin coat of Sculptamold to the hardshell surface with a spoon or putty knife. You can also use your fingers to shape the final scenic contour.

11 Foam may or may not require a final scenic coat, depending upon the type of surface texture you require. Make sure any gaps between foam layers are filled.

12 Ground cover can include various colors and textures of ground foam, as well as dirt, crushed rock, and ballast. It's available in large plastic shaker bottles as well as bags. You can also use real dirt and rocks—your yard, gravel roads or shoulders, and river banks are good sources.

13 Start by painting the surface with a thick coat of flat-finish earth-color latex paint. A cheap sponge brush is ideal for this.

14 Sprinkle the first layer of fine ground texture atop the still-wet paint. The marked area on the cork at left is a structure base.

Hardshell's greatest advantage is the ability to build steep mountains and rugged terrain rather quickly. Rolling hills are simple to create. It's easy to adjust the shape of the contours as you make the form, and it is also easy to modify the shell after it's completed by simply cutting areas away and adding new material.

The method's main disadvantage is that it's messy but less so when using plaster gauze.

Scenery surface

Make sure to provide firm, level bases for structures. Structures can sit directly upon foam, the wood table, or a scenery surface, but it's usually more realistic to elevate them by placing them on bases, **8**. Foam core or sheets of cork roadbed work well for this.

Be sure to allow for roadways. Provide a roadbed surface as you did for track, using either cork roadbed, foam, or foam core.

Modeling water

To model a simple river or lake, make sure you start with a level surface. Finish the scenery down to the banks and seal the riverbed or lakebed with a smooth layer of plaster.

Paint the surface black. To provide an illusion of depth, paint some of your base earth color along the edges and feather the earth color into the black as it goes "deeper" into the water. Glue rocks, twigs, and other details onto the waterway.

Add the simulated water. A good choice is Woodland Scenics Realistic Water, a liquid that can simply be poured into place. Make sure there's no place where the water can leak out—securely dam both ends of a river for this. Pour the Realistic Water into the waterway. A thin coat is all that's needed. Use a brush to work it around rocks and other details and along the bank. The water will level itself as it dries.

When it's dry, you can add wave effects to the surface with a coat of acrylic gloss medium or Woodland Scenics Water Effects. Apply a generous coat to the surface and then stipple and shape it with a brush to make waves. The white material will dry clear and glossy.

Water scenes add a lot of interest to both small and large layouts.

The water surface should be level and smooth. Plaster is a good base material for a riverbed or a lakebed.

Paint the riverbed flat black and then add rocks, twigs, and other material to the waterway.

Feather light earth color along the banks to simulate depth. Pour a thin coat of Realistic Water on the waterway, making sure all openings are dammed or sealed.

You need to provide a smooth surface to prep for ground cover. With hardshell, a thin coat of plaster or Sculptamold will strengthen the shell and give you a smooth surface.

Plaster (Hydrocal or plaster of paris) was long the preferred material for scenery surfaces. It's relatively inexpensive and easy to use, although it can be messy. I much prefer Sculptamold. This product is a mix of plaster and paper fiber, so it holds together without dripping, is neater to work with, and is stronger than plaster. It can be applied over wood, foam, or hardshell.

Mix Sculptamold by putting a cup or two of it in a plastic mixing bowl. Add water slowly, mixing it with a spoon, until the material is saturated but not soupy, **9**. Apply Sculptamold to the surface with a spoon, **10**. A thin coat (⅛" to ¼") is all that's needed. Work and smooth it with a putty knife, the back of a spoon, or your fingers. Keeping tools wet will keep them from sticking to the material.

Mix only as much as you can spread in 10 minutes or so. After that, the material will begin to harden. It might take a day or two to completely dry, but you can begin applying scenery materials before that.

Foam may or may not require a coat of plaster or Sculptamold. It will depend upon how finely you were able to contour the material and whether there are any cracks or seams to fill, **11**.

Scenic texturing

The most accepted way of applying scenery has become known as the water-soluble technique, first popularized by Dave Frary in his excellent book *How to Build Realistic Model Railroad Scenery* (now in its third edition, Kalmbach Books, 2005).

In a nutshell, the water-soluble technique involves painting the scenic base with earth-colored paint, adding layers of ground cover, and sealing each layer with a mix of water and white glue or matte medium. Because everything is water-based, there's no need to let one layer dry before adding the next, which greatly speeds the application process.

The method is quite forgiving. If you don't like the looks of one layer, simply add a different color or different material atop the first and keep going until you are satisfied with the appearance.

Ground foam, which is available in dozens of colors and textures, is probably the most popular choice for simulating grass and brush, **12**. Bachmann, Color Canyon, Heki, Scenic Express, Woodland Scenics, and others make a huge variety of ground foam as well as dirt, rocks, and other material. You can also use real stones and dirt from your yard or other sources.

Start with a base coat of ordinary flat interior latex house paint. Cheap paint is fine—don't waste money on the good stuff. Almost any shade of

15

An old hair-spray bottle that provides a fine mist works well for soaking the ground cover with alcohol or "wet water." Some large trigger-style bottles spray larger droplets that can disturb the materials.

16

Drip thinned glue or matte medium onto the saturated ground cover with an old contact lens solution bottle or an eyedropper. Make sure ground cover is saturated with glue.

light to dark tan will work. The key is to buy paint that dries to a flat finish, not gloss, semigloss, or satin.

Work in small areas—no more than a foot square. Use a brush to apply a thick coat of paint, working it into all pockets of the base surface—make sure no colored foam shows through, **13**.

While the paint is still wet, sprinkle on your base ground cover, **14**. Use fine materials for the first layer, varying the colors as desired. Many materials come in shaker bottles. You can also use empty parmesan cheese containers or various glass and plastic jars with holes drilled or punched in the lids.

Soak the ground material by spraying it with either "wet water"—water with a few drops of dish detergent added—or rubbing alcohol to help the glue penetrate the materials, **15**. Shield structures from the spray. You can also use a pipette or eye dropper to apply it near buildings and other detail items.

Then apply a mix of thinned white glue (about one part glue to three parts water) with an eyedropper or applicator bottle. An old contact-lens solution bottle work well as an applicator bottle. Make sure the glue saturates the ground cover, **16**.

Continue detailing the surface as you desire. You can add coarse ground foam, rocks, twigs, pockets of weeds, and other details. After each layer, reapply some glue. Secure large items, such as rocks, with full-strength white glue. For other details, apply alcohol or wet water and add more thinned white glue. The glued areas appear

17

Coarse ground foam can be applied the same way as fine foam. The Woodland Scenics field grass was cut to length, one end dipped in glue, and set in place. The trestle is built from stripwood.

white and mottled when you apply it, but the glue dries clear, **17**.

Carry the scenery right up to structures and roads. Some ground foam, dirt, or ballast against a structure base will hide the bottom of the building and will also help secure it to the scenery.

There are many other scenery techniques and materials available—too many to cover in a single chapter—including grass mats, electrostatic grass, grass tufts, and other items, **18**. Check out a hobby shop to see what's available and look through books dedicated to scenery for more detailed techniques.

Trees

Trees are vital for modeling almost every part of the country. You can buy them ready made from many manufacturers, **19**, and there are dozens of techniques for making your own. Built-up trees range from highly detailed models to less-expensive versions that simply have clumps of foam on thick plastic armatures. Save the good ones for foreground and high-visibility areas; use the cheap ones in bunches in the background.

There are dozens of ways to make your own trees. For deciduous trees, all you need is an armature (a trunk with

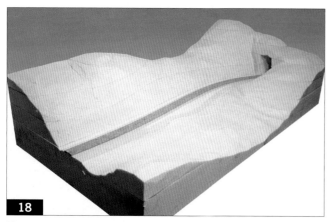

These photos show how a scene can progress from foam landform to finished scene. To capture a western desert, Pelle Søeborg applied Woodland Scenics fine ground foam and then clump foliage and field grass. The rocks are plaster castings stained with Woodland Scenics scenery colors. *Pelle Søeborg*

Many types of built-up trees are available, including this 2" Bachmann Scene Shapes Walnut (no. 32107), 3" Life-Like Scene Master Elm (no. 1974), and 2" Woodland Scenics Realistic Trees light green (no. TR1503).

To make your own trees, start by painting the armatures (trunk and branch structure) dark gray. This applies to natural materials, such as this Super Trees branch material, as well as metal or plastic armatures. *Marty McGuirk*

Soak natural-material armatures in thinned matte medium for several minutes and then hang them upside-down with a weight at the bottom (spring tweezers work well) to keep the trunks reasonably straight. *Marty McGuirk*

Add foliage material by dipping the armature in matte medium again and then sprinkling the material in place. *Marty McGuirk*

branches) and material that simulates leaf texture. Scenic Express, Woodland Scenics, and others offer kits that include armatures and foliage.

Start by painting the armature. Some kits have formed or bendable metal or plastic armatures; others use natural materials (sagebrush or other branchy plants). You can also find your own armatures—as long as they have a realistic branch structure and are the proper size. Painting an armature flat gray gives it a more realistic appearance, **20**.

With natural materials, it's important to seal and preserve the armature by soaking it for several minutes in a mix of water and matte medium (4:1 or so), **21**. Hang it upside down to dry with a weight at the bottom such as a clothespin or spring tweezers.

Add foliage material or ground foam by dipping the armature in the thinned matte medium again and then sprinkling the material in place, **22**. For solid plastic or metal armatures (which lack lacy branch structure), apply glue (such as Woodland Scenics Scenic Cement) directly to individual arms and then apply clump foliage and coarse ground foam.

A good way to "plant" trees is to drill a hole in the base of a tree, cut the head off of a straight pin or wire nail, and glue the pin or nail into the tree's base. The tree can now be pressed into place on the scenery base, **23**. (If using Sculptamold, you may have to drill a hole through it.)

The trees built by Marty McGuirk found a home on his HO layout. Marty added various shades of red and yellow foliage for a fall effect. *Marty McGuirk*

Continuing scenery to the backdrop and then adding ground foam at the base of it will help hide the joint between the backdrop and layout table.

Walthers' HO street sections make it easy to realistically model city scenes. After painting roads an appropriate concrete or asphalt color, add painted cracks and patches, and follow with powdered chalk weathering.

26 This HO gravel road is a mix of Woodland Scenics fine brown and buff ballast. The truck is from Mini-Metals, and the sign and wood grade-crossing kit are by Blair Line.

27 Start by spreading a layer of ballast between the rails. A soft, flat brush works well for distributing the ballast evenly between the ties.

28 Build up a shoulder of ballast outside of each rail along the roadbed, again shaping it with a brush.

29 At turnouts, make sure the ballast is clear of guardrails, points, frogs, and throw bars.

Backdrops

Even a simple backdrop will dramatically improve the appearance of a layout by blocking the view of a wall or room. Paint the backdrop a light sky blue color. Common household acrylic interior flat paint will do the job.

Apply the scenery all the way to the backdrop and up onto it slightly. Spread some matte medium or white glue along the bottom of the backdrop and then press ground foam into it, **24**. This will help hide the edge where the scenery meets the backdrop. Placing buildings and trees along the backdrop will also help hide the edge.

If you want to detail a backdrop, a good resource is Mike Danneman's book *Painting Backdrops for Your Model Railroad* (Kalmbach Books, 2008).

Roads

Making a paved road is a matter of putting a smooth surface down and then painting and weathering it to resemble asphalt or concrete. For a high level of detail, Walthers offers plastic components for city streets in HO, including sidewalks and curbs (see some in photo on page 58). Rix makes injection-molded simulated concrete-slab straight highway sections in N and HO that look great. Busch, Faller, and Noch make flexible roadway material in HO and N scale that can be secured to a smooth surface, and Mini Highways and S&S Hobby Products make straight, intersection, and curved roadway sections in HO and N.

Paint concrete roads with colors such as Polly Scale Concrete or Aged Concrete, and asphalt roads with Polly Scale Grimy Black (or a lighter flat gray color). Add cracks and tar repairs with a fine brush and black paint and weather the roads with various shades of gray and black powdered chalk, **25**.

Gravel roads can be made with fine rock or ballast, **26**. Spread tan or buff ballast along the road surface, using a brush to smooth and shape it. Soak it with rubbing alcohol (applied either with a fine mist sprayer or dribbled on gently with a pipette). Follow by bonding it with a glue/water mix as was done with the rest of the scenery.

Ballasting track

Real track sits on a bed of crushed rock called ballast. Several manufacturers make scale ballast, including Arizona Rock & Mineral, Bachmann, Busch, Highball, and Woodland Scenics. I recommend fine ballast for N and HO scales, medium for S, and medium or coarse for O scale.

Prototype ballast comes in a variety of colors depending upon its source, from shades of gray to deep red to brown. Individual rocks are rarely uniform in color, so having

30 After wetting the ballast with alcohol or wet water, soak the ballast thoroughly with a thinned mix of white glue. Hold the dispenser close to the track to avoid disturbing the ballast.

31 A cotton swab works well for soaking up excess glue on ties at turnout points and throw bars. Move the points back and forth as the glue dries to ensure they don't become stuck in place.

32 Mix ballast with ground foam to get a weedy, grown-over appearance on spurs and other seldom-used tracks.

33 You can apply ballast over all-in-one track in the same manner as regular track and roadbed.

some variation in model ballast adds to realism. You can mix multiple colors to get this effect.

Start by spreading a layer of ballast between the rails. Use a wide, soft brush to spread the ballast evenly between the ties, **27**. Do the same on the outside of the rails along the ties and then add ballast to form a shoulder along the side of the roadbed, **28**. Use the brush again to shape the profile. Do this to a couple of feet of track at a time. Then sweep ballast from turnouts at guardrails with a paintbrush, **29**.

On real railroads, generally the more traffic a line sees, the more maintenance it receives, and the neater the ballast profile is. Don't worry about having every piece of ballast in order—the prototype certainly doesn't. Freshly ballasted (or reballasted) track sometimes has a lot of ballast covering ties; on other lines, every tie can be seen.

Fix the ballast by first soaking it with rubbing alcohol. A fine-mist sprayer usually won't disturb ballast; you can also use a pipette to soak the area. Apply a mix of glue and water as you did with other scenery, **30**. Apply it generously—make sure the glue saturates the ballast completely.

Soak up any glue around turnout points and throw bars with a cotton swab, **31**. As the glue is drying, move the throw bar back and forth a few times to make sure it doesn't get glued in place.

When the glue dries, go over the track with a track cleaning block to remove glue residue from the rails. Run a test car over the track and remove any ballast stuck inside the rails with tweezers so it doesn't interfere with wheel flanges.

For a more realistic appearance, you can vary the ballast on sidings and spur tracks. Spurs are often overgrown

and weedy. I mixed cinder ballast with green ground foam and applied it to a spur, **32**, covering up several ties in the process. You can do this to any extreme—just make sure that the track is passable for rolling stock.

You can also ballast all-in-one track for a better appearance, **33**. Follow the same steps as described and just treat the plastic roadbed as if it were cork. Painting the beveled edge of the roadbed with white glue prior to adding ballast will help it remain in place.

Layout details

Even when the track and structures are in place and the scenery is finished, a layout is far from complete. What makes a model railroad come to life is the myriad details and scenes that you can add to it. Figures, vehicles, signs, telegraph poles, and other details can always be added. Turn the page and we'll look at the trains themselves.

1

CHAPTER TEN
Selecting locomotives

Today, modelers can operate a variety of outstanding steam and diesel locomotive models, including from top left, an Athearn Genesis HO Northern Pacific EMD F9, an Atlas HO Union Pacific EMD SD24, a Kato N scale EMD E8, a Fox Valley Models N scale GE ES44AC, and a Proto Heritage N scale Norfolk & Western Y-3 2-8-8-2 steam locomotive.

Model railroaders today are blessed with a tremendous selection of highly detailed, smooth-running locomotive models, 1. It wasn't that long ago that getting such a model involved the expense and trouble of adding a bunch of after-market details as well as having to do a comprehensive mechanical tune-up. Having a basic understanding of how real locomotives work can help you decide which model locomotives you should choose. We'll take a look at both steam and diesel locomotives and then look at the characteristics of good models.

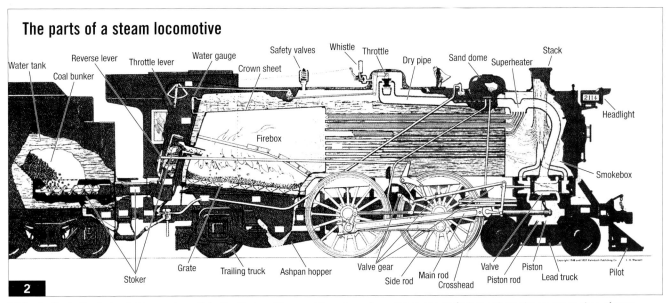

The parts of a steam locomotive

Water tank
Coal bunker
Reverse lever
Throttle lever
Water gauge
Crown sheet
Safety valves
Whistle
Throttle
Dry pipe
Sand dome
Superheater
Stack
Headlight
Firebox
Smokebox
2114

Stoker
Grate
Trailing truck
Ashpan hopper
Valve gear
Side rod
Main rod
Crosshead
Valve
Piston
Piston rod
Lead truck
Pilot

2

Water in the boiler is heated by coal or oil in the firebox. The resulting steam is routed to the cylinders, where the steam pushes pistons connected to the drivers. Steam locomotives were powerful, but required more maintenance than diesel locomotives.

Steam locomotives

Steam locomotives dominated railroading into the 1940s. Their size and power grew over time: many locomotives of the 1930s and '40s put out more than 5,000 horsepower and could haul mile-long freight trains at high speeds.

The basic workings of a steam locomotive are shown in figure **2**. A fire in the firebox, fueled by coal or oil, heats water in the boiler. As the water boils and turns to steam, it is captured at the top of the steam dome. Opening the throttle allows the steam to move into cylinders ahead of the driving wheels on each side of the locomotive. The steam moves large pistons that push rods connected to the driving wheels, or drivers. The steam is then exhausted from the cylinders through the smokebox and out the smokestack.

The pilot wheels at the front of the locomotive help guide and stabilize the locomotive through curves, and the rear (trailing) truck helps support the weight of the firebox. The tender, pulled directly behind the locomotive, carries water and fuel (coal or oil).

Steam locomotives were designed for specific types of service. Switching locomotives (switchers), which worked at slow speeds in yards, typically had no pilot or trailing wheels and had fairly low (small-diameter) drivers. High-speed passenger locomotives often had four-wheel pilot trucks for

3

Chicago, Burlington & Quincy 4-8-4 (Northern) No. 5629 is an example of a powerful, modern steam locomotive. Its primary duty was hauling fast freight trains. *David P. Morgan Library*

stability and tall drivers for generating speed. Freight locomotives typically had two-wheel pilot trucks and lower drivers to generate more tractive effort but operated at slower speeds.

Locomotive types are indicated by their wheel arrangement in the Whyte system (see page 77), designated by the total number of pilot wheels, drivers, and trailing wheels. In addition, most locomotive types also have nicknames to identify them. For example, a common freight locomotive was the 2-8-2, which was also known as a Mikado, and the 4-6-2 Pacific was standard passenger power into the 1930s.

Larger locomotives began appearing in the 1930s, taking advantage of bigger boilers and higher steam pressure to get more power. The 4-6-4 Hudson became popular for passenger service with the larger 4-8-4 Northern (commonly called a Dixie in the south)

handling heavier passenger as well as freight trains, **3**.

Articulated locomotives had two engines (and two sets of drivers) under the boiler. These have an extra number in the classification representing the additional drivers. Into the early 1900s, articulated locomotives were small, built for tight curves and steep grades. Articulateds soon evolved into large, powerful locomotives built for hauling heavy, slow "drag" freights. Modern articulateds served in fast freight and passenger service, best demonstrated by the Union Pacific's well-known Challenger (4-6-6-4) and Big Boy (4-8-8-4) locomotives, which operated well into the 1950s.

Steam details

Steam locomotives were not off-the-shelf items—each order was custom-built by manufacturers, including the

Union Pacific No. 5427 is a General Electric ES44AC. It's an example of a modern 4,400-horsepower six-axle diesel common in mainline service today.

Today's models feature finer detail and smoother operation than those of the 1980s and '90s. This HO Proto 2000 F3 includes a cab interior, separate grab irons, prototype-specific fans, and antenna.

N scale locomotives are also much improved from those of the past, with finer detail and factory-installed DCC and sound. This is an N scale Athearn model of an EMD FP45.

Removing the shell on this HO scale Proto 1000 RS-2 requires unscrewing the coupler box from each end and slipping the box out through the opening in the pilot.

With the couplers off, the shell of the RS-2 simply slides off the chassis. Be careful not to damage handrails and other details.

The shell of this N scale Bachmann F-M H-16-44 slides off the chassis with the couplers still in place.

American Locomotive Company (Alco), Baldwin, and Lima, or by the railroads themselves. Locomotives of different classes did not use common components. Thus, one railroad's 4-6-2s might look completely different than another's (except for the wheel arrangement).

Exceptions to this were locomotives built under the direction of the United States Railroad Administration (USRA), which assumed control of U.S. railroads during World War I. USRA locomotives of several wheel arrangements (and later copies made by several builders) served on multiple railroads.

Steam spotting features varied by railroad and era. Differences included the style of the cab; the size and shape of the boiler; valve-gear type; the style of drivers and other wheels; and the style, size, and shape of the tender. Detail differences included bells, whistles, headlights, number boxes, pilots, running board location, and air pumps.

Diesel locomotives

Diesel locomotives first became popular as switchers in the 1930s and then as high-speed passenger locomotives powering early streamliners in the early and mid-1930s. The introduction of

Electro-Motive Corporation's FT in 1939 brought the diesel to heavy mainline freight service, a job diesels would gradually take from steam throughout the 1940s. By the mid-1950s, most steam locomotives had been relegated to the scrap line.

Diesels were more expensive than comparable steam locomotives but gained an advantage in availability, operating costs, and repair costs. Unlike steam locomotives, each manufacturer's diesels were off-the-shelf models with common components among models—much like automobiles. Other than some optional features, one railroad's GP9s were essentially the same as any other railroad's.

Although usually simply called diesels, these locomotives are technically diesel-electrics. A large diesel engine turns a generator or alternator, which provides electricity to power electric (traction) motors mounted on the axles.

Most modern diesels are large locomotives, 4,400 or more horse-power, and ride on a pair of three-axle trucks, **4**. Early diesels were smaller (the FT was 1,350 horsepower) and had four or six axles.

A fundamental advantage of diesel operation is the ability to couple two or more locomotives together under the control of a single engineer (called multiple units). This allows adding or subtracting locomotives as needed based on train size.

Early passenger and road freight diesels featured a streamlined carbody style of construction (called cab units), with a truss framework integral to the strength of the body (see the E and F units in photo **1**). Although attractive, engine access was difficult, which made many maintenance duties difficult.

The road switcher became the dominant locomotive style by the mid-1950s. These locomotives are utilitarian in design, looking like stretched-out versions of switchers. The engine is under the long hood, with access doors along the side. Running boards (walk-ways) follow each side, with a cab and short nose at one end.

Diesel models

You'll find varying quality in model locomotives in terms of both detail and operation, but by and large, today's model offerings are a far cry from what was available 15 or 20 years ago, **5**. Most of today's models run smoothly with excellent low-speed characteristics. Many feature a variety of separately applied details, including railroad-specific items.

Digital Command Control (DCC) decoders now come standard (or as options) in many model locomotives. On many models, sound and lighting effects are available as standard or as options.

High-quality diesels are available from Athearn Genesis (HO and N), Atlas (O, HO, and N), Fox Valley

10

Typical HO diesel construction is shown by the Proto 1000 RS-2, which has the motor in the middle with twin flywheels, universal joints to each truck, and a circuit board atop the frame.

11

Many N scale diesels, such as this Bachmann Fairbanks-Morse model, have large weights surrounding the motor and other components.

12

This HO Proto 2000 E6 model has a decoder and sound unit taking up much of the space on top of the chassis, with the motor and drive train hidden from view.

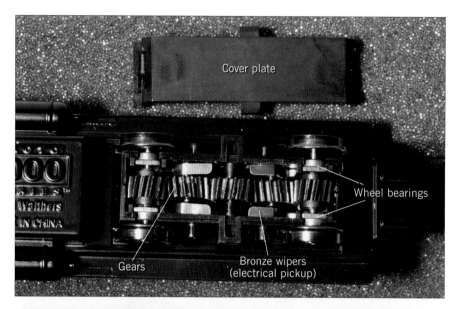

Small tabs hold the truck cover plates in place on the Proto 1000 HO RS-2 (top) and a Bachmann N scale model. Add a bit of grease to the gears (the Bachmann model was overlubricated at the factory) and a drop of oil to each wheel bearing.

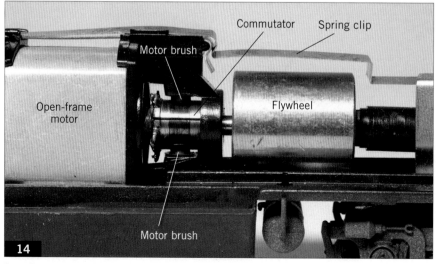

Open-frame motors have the commutator and brushes exposed. The commutator is dirty (the vertical black streak) on this older Athearn HO model.

Models (N), InterMountain (HO and N), Micro-Trains (N and Z), MTH (HO, O) Proto 2000 (HO), Proto N (N), S-Helper Service (S), and Stewart (HO). Good-quality diesels (but without some of the detailing of higher-end models) can be found from Athearn Ready-To-Roll (HO and N), Atlas Trainman, Bachmann Spectrum (HO, N), Proto 1000 (HO and N), and Walthers Trainline (HO).

There are several things to look for when buying model locomotives. Diesels should have all axles powered and all wheels picking up electricity. Many train-set quality locomotives (and lots of older engines) have just half their axles powered and half their wheels picking up power (see Chapter 1). The result is a rougher ride as these models are more susceptible to dirty track. Many of these models also have poor-quality motors that are less powerful and don't respond to speed changes well.

Check the details on the model. Better models have numbers in number boards, individual grab irons, and separately applied horns, bells, antennas, windshield wipers, and other details along with accurate paint schemes and fine lettering, **6**. Many of today's models have details to match specific road names. Low-end models have more parts molded in place with out-of-scale (or otherwise inaccurate) details, and many sport paint schemes that are poorly done or don't accurately represent a real locomotive.

If you're thinking about going with DCC, consider models with factory-installed decoders. This saves you the installation work, and the price is usually comparable to buying a separate after-market decoder.

Remember the curves of your track when buying diesel models. On sharp curves (9¾"-radius in N, 18" in HO, and 36" in O), four-axle diesels will look and operate best. Large, modern six-axle diesels will look and run better on medium- and broad-radius curves.

Diesel construction

It's a good idea not to disassemble locomotives unless you absolutely have to. However, occasionally you'll need to get

15

To clean the commutator, rub it gently with an eraser while rotating the driveshaft by hand.

16

Run the back edge of a hobby knife through each gap in the commutator to remove any debris from the eraser.

17

The black streak is now gone, and the commutator is back to its original brass color.

Whyte system

The Whyte system classifies steam locomotives by wheel arrangement (pilot wheels/drivers/trailing wheels). This list is not inclusive, but it reflects the most common locomotive types. Names reflect the most common usage although some railroads used different terms.

Type	Side arrangement	Name	Service
0-4-0	<00		Switcher
0-6-0	<000		Switcher
0-8-0	<0000		Switcher
2-6-0	<o000	Mogul	Freight
2-6-2	<o000o	Prairie	Freight
2-8-0	<o0000	Consolidation	Freight
2-8-2	<o0000o	Mikado	Freight
2-8-4	<o0000oo	Berkshire	Freight
2-10-0	<o00000	Decapod	Freight
2-10-2	<o00000o	Santa Fe	Freight
2-10-4	<o00000oo	Texas	Freight
2-6-6-6	<o000 000ooo	Allegheny	Freight
2-8-8-4	<o0000 0000oo	Yellowstone	Freight
4-4-0	<oo00	American	Passenger
4-4-2	<oo00o	Atlantic	Passenger
4-6-0	<oo000	Ten-Wheeler	Passenger
4-6-2	<oo000o	Pacific	Passenger
4-6-4	<oo000oo	Hudson	Passenger
4-8-2	<oo0000o	Mountain *	Dual
4-8-4	<oo00000o	Northern **	Dual
4-10-2	<oo00000o	Southern Pacific	Dual
4-12-2	<oo000000o	Union Pacific	Freight
4-6-6-4	<oo000 000oo	Challenger	Dual
4-8-8-4	<oo0000 0000oo	Big Boy	Freight

* called Mohawks on the New York Central
** called Dixies by many Southern railroads

inside the shell to do some maintenance. Keep the manufacturers' instruction manuals and guides for all of your locomotives—I put all of mine in a folder in my workshop. You'll find these handy for a number of reasons, especially if the locomotive is factory-equipped with a decoder and/or sound unit.

Most diesels follow the same basic construction design, but the shell-removal process varies greatly. Check the instructions and/or an exploded construction diagram first. For some, removing the shell requires unscrewing the coupler pockets from each end, **7**

and **8**. Other models have screws under the frame that pass through holes in the frame into the shell. Some models have shells with tabs that snap in place on the frame, requiring the shell to be squeezed inward and pulled up off of the frame. The shells on many N scale diesels simply slide off the chassis, **9**.

Contemporary models have the motor near the center of the frame, but electrically isolated from the frame, **10**. A large weight, or two halves of a weight, surround the motor, **11**. You'll find a flywheel at one or both ends of the motor, mounted on the drive shaft. These help

smooth operation—as they spin, their momentum keeps the driveshaft spinning for a bit even if the power stops.

A universal joint carries the driveshaft rotation to a worm gear atop each truck tower. From there, a series of gears in each truck tower transfers the motion down to each axle of the truck.

Metal wipers (usually sprung bronze) pick up electricity from each wheel, with a wire from each truck sideframe carrying the power to a circuit board atop the weight. This circuit board also provides a connection point to the lights, and on some locomotives,

18

This HO Proto 2000 USRA 0-6-0 switcher is typical of the highly detailed steam locomotive models now available. The model also has a DCC decoder with sound installed in the tender.

19

Bachmann offers this N scale model of a USRA light Mountain (4-8-2) in its Spectrum line.

it holds circuitry for constant-intensity or reversing headlights.

Many models in HO and larger scales have a socket on the circuit board to allow a plug-in DCC decoder (more on those in Chapter 7). If the model is already equipped with DCC, or DCC and sound, the circuit board will include the decoder, with speakers within the weight and frame, **12**.

Diesel maintenance

Today's models require only periodic lubrication to keep them running smoothly. New models are usually lubricated at the factory; in fact, many models are overlubricated. Take a look at the underside of each truck and under each sideframe. If you see oil oozing out, use the corner of a cloth or paper towel to remove as much of it as you can.

After that, most models will only require lubrication once a year or so—more often if you run models

frequently. If a model starts behaving erratically, or it starts to squeak or squeal, it's likely time to lube it.

Some models have cover plates under the trucks that can be removed to reveal the truck gears, while others have a small hole in this plate to allow access, **13**. Add a drop of plastic-compatible light grease (such as LaBelle no. 106) to just one gear—the gears will transfer the lube to each other as they move. Then apply a drop of plastic-compatible light oil (such as LaBelle no. 108) to each axle bearing and the bearings for the worm gear.

Don't apply too much grease or oil! Excess lubrication will attract dust, dirt, carpet fibers, hair, and other stray material. As you're lubricating a model, check for stray material and clean it out before adding oil or grease.

Next, turn your attention to the motor. Motors come in two styles: enclosed or open-frame. Open-frame

motors have the commutator and brushes exposed at one end, **14**. Many older models such as the Athearn model in the photo have a more spartan interior appearance than newer models. A key difference in these models is that the frame is used to carry power from one rail to the motor by direct contact with the motor housing. This becomes important if you want to add a decoder, as the motor must be isolated from the frame. That goes beyond the scope of this book, but Mike Polsgrove's book *DCC Projects & Applications* (Kalmbach Books, 2006) covers many DCC issues.

The commutator must be clean for the motor to operate smoothly. If carbon deposits build up on it, operation can become jerky or erratic. Check the commutator by examining it. It should be a brass color, so if it is darkened around the outside, it's time to clean it.

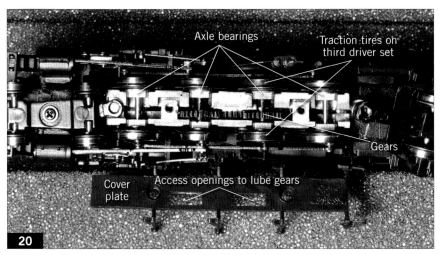

The cover plate on the Bachmann N 4-8-2 is held in place by two small screws. Removing the plate provides access to gears and bearings.

Horn-hook couplers were standard on HO equipment into the 1990s. Replace them with knuckle couplers.

One of the easiest ways is to use an eraser or the corner of an abrasive track-cleaning block to scrub it. Rotate the drive shaft by hand and gently rub the commutator until the carbon buildup disappears, **15**. Make sure the thin gaps in the commutator are clean by running the tip of a hobby knife through each gap, **16**. When you're done, clean it with a cotton swab dipped in alcohol, **17**. Use some canned air to blow out any debris from the area.

Steam locomotives

Today's high-quality steam locomotives have an incredible amount of detail: look for separately applied items such as piping, bell, whistle, bell cord, and pumps, and blackened rods and valve gear, **18**. There's a much bigger variety of locomotives offered as well, **19**.

As with diesels, the more wheels that pick up power, the better. Many steam locomotives use tender wheels for this as well as drivers.

Steam locomotives can be tricky to disassemble—fortunately, there are few reasons to do so. As with diesels, check the manufacturer's instructions and illustrated diagrams. The boiler/cab is sometimes held in place with a screw or screws hidden atop the boiler (in the stack or under the steam dome or sandbox) or underneath the chassis.

Many older steam models have the motor and flywheel in the cab, with the motor angled downward so the worm contacts a worm gear attached to one of the driving axles. Some models have gears connecting all drivers; others rely on the side rods to transfer power to the other axles.

Some models have a plate under the locomotive that can be removed to gain access to the axle bearings and any gears, **20**. As with diesels, a drop of light oil on the bearings is about all that's needed for maintenance. This photo shows the rubber traction tires on one driver set of a Bachmann N scale 4-8-2. This is common on N scale steam locomotives to boost tractive effort, since they have less room inside for weight compared to diesels.

Newer steam models tend to have detailed cab interiors, so the motor is moved forward into the boiler. Space is tight in there, and unless a model has a major breakdown, it's wise to just leave things in place.

Many steam models rely on tender wheels to help with electrical contact, and many have circuit boards, decoders, and speakers in the tender as well. Power on these models is transferred between tender and locomotive by a plug-and-socket connection. Check the owner's manual for each model.

As with diesels, large steam locomotives may have problems operating on tight curves. Stick to reasonably small models—no bigger than 4-6-2 or 2-8-2—unless you have medium or broad curves. Some larger models (including articulateds) will run on tight curves, but the overhang of the boiler front and cab will look awkward.

Couplers

Into the 1990s, almost all HO models came factory-equipped with horn-hook couplers, **21**, and N scale models had Rapido couplers (see Chapter 11). Both suffered in appearance (they didn't look anything like a real coupler) as well as operation: they coupled well but were difficult to uncouple manually and nearly impossible to uncouple automatically.

Through that period, the Kadee Magne-Matic coupler (HO, S, and O scales) and Micro-Trains Magne-Matic (N and Z scales) were the de facto standard for serious modelers, most of whom immediately swapped out the original couplers when buying a new locomotive or car. These are realistic in appearance and operate very well.

During the 1990s, many companies came out with their own compatible automatic knuckle couplers, and most models now come from the manufacturer equipped with knuckle couplers. If you run across an older model with one of the old couplers, you can simply swap it for a new version. Micro-Trains and Kadee both have extensive online conversion guides that list the replacement coupler to mount on various manufacturers' models. Go to www.micro-trains.com and www.kadee.com for details. Kadee offers the no. 13 sample kit in HO, which includes one each of 25 different couplers—these are a great help in fitting new couplers to existing models. See Chapter 11 for information on replacing couplers.

1

CHAPTER ELEVEN

Running rolling stock

High-quality freight cars are available in every scale, including this InterMountain HO Peavey covered hopper, Athearn HO Bay Colony boxcar, Accurail HO USRA Baltimore & Ohio twin hopper, Atlas HO Fuelane pressure tank car, Micro-Trains N Southern enclosed auto rack, Red Caboose HO Illinois Central boxcar, and ExactRail N Canadian National boxcar.

Freight and passenger cars, called rolling stock, are the heart of a model railroad, 1. The selection of freight cars by road name or type can show a lot about your railroad, including the region modeled, type of traffic hauled, and era of your layout.

Manufacturers offer hundreds of different cars, each with a variety of road names and paint schemes. Because of this variety, many beginners (as well as experienced modelers) succumb to the temptation of acquiring cars on a whim, just because they bear an attractive paint scheme or unusual design.

However, once you get further into the hobby, you will discover that a colorful 1920s-era billboard refrigerator car just doesn't look right coupled to a modern 89-foot-long auto-rack car. Understanding what each type of prototype car does and learning how cars have evolved over time will help you choose a good mix of rolling stock that makes sense for the period you decide to model.

Freight cars

The boxcar has been the basic freight car since the beginning of railroading, **2**. Boxcars are used for hauling just about anything that can be packed in a box or crate, along with plenty of other goods. Boxcars were also the primary car for carrying autos through the 1950s and for carrying bulk grain through the 1960s. Insulated plug-door boxcars began appearing in the 1960s, **3**.

Most cars featured wood construction with steel frames and outside bracing into the 1930s. All-steel cars of various designs became common from the mid-1930s onward. Forty feet was the standard length through the 1950s (although automobile cars and some others were longer, when 50- and 60-foot cars became common.

Refrigerator cars. Refrigerator cars, also called reefers, are used to haul fruits and vegetables, frozen goods, beer, and many other temperature-sensitive products, **4**. Their basic appearance is like a boxcar, but with swinging plug doors on early cars and sliding plug doors on modern cars. Most featured wood bodies into the 1940s, with 36- and 40-foot cars being common.

Ice was used to keep loads cool into the 1960s. Bunkers at each end of the car held crushed ice, which was added via hatches on the roof atop each bunker. Mechanical refrigeration units began appearing in large numbers in the 1950s, spurred on by the frozen-food industry, and today, all reefers rely on mechanical units except for a handful of cryogenic cars.

Hoppers and gondolas. Hopper cars have bottom discharge outlets and carry bulk products such as coal and aggregates. Small two-bay cars were common through the 1950s, with

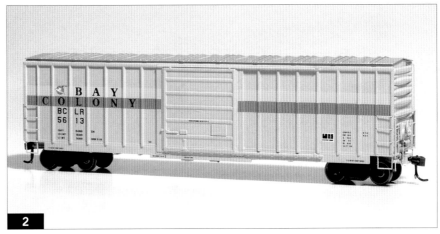

2 This HO Athearn Genesis model is patterned after a prototype 50-foot boxcar built by SIECO in the 1970s and 1980s. The model has many separately applied details, including grab irons and brake gear.

3 Eastern Seaboard Models makes this N scale Pacific Car & Foundry/Magor 40-foot insulated plug-door boxcar. It's lettered for Conrail in a restenciled ex-Penn Central paint scheme.

4 Refrigerator car models in HO include this 1940s-era, 40-foot ice-bunker car from InterMountain (front) and a 1960s 57-foot mechanical reefer from Athearn with some extra details added.

5

The Micro-Trains N scale hopper at front is based on a panel-side, two-bay 1930s prototype, while the DeLuxe Innovations car at rear is a Bethgon Coalporter, a modern coal gondola.

6

These N scale models include a Trainworx GS gondola and a Bluford Shops model of a New York Central 70-ton, three-bay hopper.

7

Athearn Genesis makes this HO model of one of the most common modern grain cars, a Trinity 5,161-cubic-foot covered hopper. It has etched-metal running boards and many extra details.

8

This Walthers Gold Line HO model is patterned after a modern Funnel-Flow tank car (the middle is lower than the ends) in molten sulfur service.

9

Micro-Trains makes N scale models of 1960s and 1970s 89-foot open auto-rack cars as well as modern enclosed auto racks.

10

The prototype of this Walthers HO model is a Pullman sleeping car used on the New York Central's flagship *20th Century Limited* passenger train.

11

The style of this "beaver-tail" observation car, an HO model by Fox Valley Models, was unique to the Milwaukee Road, built in 1935 for the railroad's *Hiawatha*.

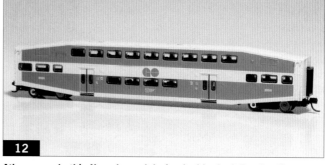

12

Athearn made this N scale model of a double-deck Bombardier commuter coach, lettered in Toronto's GO Transit scheme.

13

Horn-hook couplers were standard on HO rolling stock into the 1990s. They were ugly and not known for operating well.

14

Rapido N scale couplers, standard into the 1990s, were designed to slide over each other to couple. They are oversize, unrealistic, and difficult to uncouple.

15

Kadee couplers have long been popular for appearance and operation. This is a scale-size Kadee no. 58 HO coupler mounted on an Accurail stock car.

16

The HO scale Kadee no. 5 and many other similar couplers rely on a separate bronze centering spring in the coupler pocket.

17

Some couplers rely on integral springs on each side of the shank to center the coupler, such as this HO Bachmann E-Z Mate (left), shown in an Accurail freight car, and the Kadee no. 147 "whisker" spring coupler.

larger three- and four-bay cars after that, **5** and **6**.

Large "bathtub" gondolas resemble hopper cars and are used most often in unit coal train service. These cars have no bottom outlets and are instead unloaded by rotary dumpers. Other gondolas can be found hauling just about anything, including steel, scrap metal, aggregates, machinery, rolls of coiled steel, and pipe.

Covered hoppers were developed in the 1930s to carry bulk goods such as sand, cement, and carbon black. By the 1960s, they began hauling grain, **7**, and now are among the most common cars on the rails. They also carry fertilizer, plastic pellets, and many other products.

Tank cars. Tank cars carry a tremendous variety of liquids including fuels and chemicals, along with many food-grade products such as corn syrup and vegetable oil, **8**. Cars with capacities of 8,000 to 10,000 gallons were typical into the 1950s. Car sizes have since grown and are based on the density of products they are designed to

carry, with some 60-foot cars topping out at 33,000 gallons.

Flatcars. Flatcars include general-purpose cars that carry machinery and bulk goods and specialized cars such as center-beam lumber cars, auto racks, **9**, and several types of intermodal cars for carrying trailers and containers.

Into the early diesel era, many railroads emblazoned their cars with large heralds, railroad initials, or road names. Many railroads employed cars as advertising for their passenger trains, with train names or slogans. Freight car paint schemes became simpler over time, and with the demise of railroad-operated passenger trains, single-color schemes with simple graphics became more common.

Passenger cars

Passenger cars have evolved in similar fashion to freight cars. Into the early 1900s, most were wood, but by World War I, steel had become the preferred material for safety and durability reasons. Passenger cars were longer than freight cars, with common lengths to

80 feet. These steel cars built through the 1930s were known as heavyweights because their steel body on steel frame construction could make them weigh in at 70 or more tons. Many rode on six-wheel trucks.

These cars gave way to streamlined, lightweight cars starting in the 1930s, **10**. Builders such as ACF, Pullman, and Budd began building cars from stainless steel, aluminum, and other lighter-weight materials for the new diesel streamliners that were going into service. Cars were still up to 85 feet long, but they weighed much less at around 50 or 60 tons.

There are many types of passenger cars. Featuring rows of seats for passengers, coaches and chair cars are the most common. Diners contained a kitchen as well as tables for serving meals. Lounges featured seating areas with bar (and sometimes snack) service. Sleeping cars came in a variety of configurations, with separate sleeping compartments in a range of sizes.

Many trains had observation cars that were designed to be placed at the

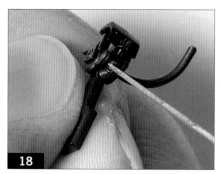

18 To replace a knuckle spring, fit a knife blade between the coils. Place it over one mounting peg and then compress the coils and fit the other end over the other mounting peg.

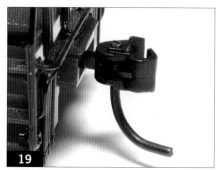

19 Some couplers use integral plastic knuckle springs. Avoid these, as they can take a set and lose their spring action.

20 The Accumate coupler is in two halves, each with a spring. The hole is for mounting the uncoupling pin.

21 This is Kadee's HO scale coupler mounting gauge. The top of the car's coupler should be the same height as the top of the coupler on the gauge.

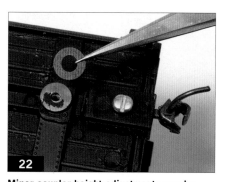

22 Minor coupler height adjustments can be made by adding a thin washer between the truck and car bolster.

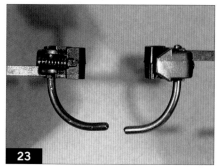

23 Couplers are made with overset and underset shanks. These are Kadee HO no. 41 and no. 49 couplers.

end of the train, **11**. These were generally coach or lounge cars that had an enhanced viewing area toward the rear. Dome cars became popular starting in the 1940s, with a viewing area projecting above the standard roofline. Double-deck cars, introduced by the Santa Fe in the 1950s, evolved to the standard for long-distance cars operated today by Amtrak. Many commuter agencies also operate double-deck cars, **12**.

Baggage cars carried mail, parcels, and express merchandise as well as passengers' baggage, and Railway Post Office (RPO) cars had working post office areas for sorting mail. A combine (combination) car was part coach and part baggage or mail car.

The number and type of cars in any given passenger train varied widely by railroad and route. A local that stopped at all stations along the line might have just two or three coaches. Mixed trains were common on branch and secondary lines into the 1960s. These were local freight trains with a rider coach or combine at the end.

An intermediate overnight train might have a mix of coaches and sleepers with a lounge or diner. Some luxury passenger trains didn't have coaches, only sleeping cars, a lounge, diner, and observation car.

Railroads operated their own passenger trains until the coming of Amtrak in 1971. Until that time, passenger cars by and large stayed on their home railroads (unlike freight cars, which roam around the country).

Passenger trains gradually decreased in number from the 1950s through the 1960s. The coming of Amtrak consolidated U.S. intercity passenger operations under a single governing body (commuter trains in large cities are usually operated by a local authority).

Freight car models

Modelers in all scales have a variety of good-quality freight cars from which to choose. Most cars today are available in ready-to-run form, with all details in place and trucks and couplers installed and ready for service.

This is a dramatic change from even a few years ago. Into the mid-1990s, most high-quality rolling stock was only available in kit form—the bulk of ready-to-run equipment was inexpensive, low-quality train-set-type cars.

You can still find kits for many freight cars, generally at a lower price than ready-to-run cars, and you can still find a lot of older kits on eBay, at swap meets, and from various dealers. You'll have to decide for yourself which you prefer.

As with locomotive models, cars are available with differing levels of added detail (which usually correspond with price). At the high end are freight cars from Athearn Genesis (HO, N), Atlas (HO, N), Atlas O (O), Bluford Shops (N), Branchline Trains (HO), DeLuxe Innovations (N), Eastern Seaboard Models (N), ExactRail (HO, N), Fox Valley Models (N), InterMountain (HO and N), Kadee (HO), Kato (HO), Micro-Trains (N, Z), Proto 2000 (HO), Red Caboose (HO, N), Trainworx (HO, N), and Walthers Gold Line

(HO). Other good models, but not as detailed include Accurail Accuready (HO), Athearn Ready-To-Roll (HO), Proto 1000, and Walthers Trainline (HO, N).

If you're interested in building your own kits, you can still get them from Accurail (HO), A-Line (HO), Bowser (HO, N), Branchline (HO), Red Caboose (HO, N), and others.

In judging the quality of a car, look for separate stirrup steps and grab irons (which are formed wire, not plastic, on better cars). Check the running boards (roofwalks)—better cars have these etched in metal or molded in thin-profile plastic. Older models will have thick plastic parts with no see-through detail.

Look for metal wheels, knuckle couplers, uncoupling levers, brake hoses, separate brake gear (including the reservoir, control valve, and cylinder with separate piping under the car), and a brake wheel with fine cross-sections and detail.

Even if you don't notice these things readily now, your eye will become more and more aware as you gain experience in the hobby. Over time, you'll appreciate models with better, more-realistic details.

Car mix

As noted earlier, it's easy to just start buying freight car models that look good, without regard to era or prototype. As you figure out details of what you like and what you want to model, you'll probably find yourself narrowing down your focus. Most experienced model railroaders model a specific period (a year, month, or even week).

You don't have to do this, of course, but I suggest keeping cars to the same general era for the most realistic effect. The nice thing is that freight cars have long service lives, and many cars run 30 to 40 years before being retired. That means that even if you decide to model, say, 1970, you can still have some cars built in the 1940s rolling on your layout.

Freight cars don't stay just on their own railroad's property—they roam throughout the North American rail system. The percentages of home road

Automatic and delayed-action uncoupling

Automatic knuckle couplers can be uncoupled by magnets mounted on or under the track. Several types of uncoupling magnets are available from Kadee and others. Some are designed to be placed temporarily atop the ties between the rails as needed. Others can be permanently installed either below the ties (you'll have to know where they're needed before laying track) or by cutting away the ties and gluing it in place. Another type, the electromagnet, is only activated when power is supplied to it.

The magnets work by pulling the uncoupling pins of coupled cars outward to open the knuckles and separate them. Cars will uncouple only when there is slack between them. If the couplers are taut—as when a train is being pulled—the cars will stay coupled.

It's a good idea to install permanent magnets only on side tracks and spurs and not on main lines, where accidental uncoupling—such as when a train slows down and the slack happens to run in over a magnet—can cause serious disruptions to operations. On main lines, use either a portable magnet or an electromagnet.

Delayed-action uncoupling provides the ability to uncouple a car at one spot and push it to any location on a track beyond the uncoupling magnet. This allows you to have just one uncoupler per spur track, even if you'll want to spot cars at multiple locations on it.

Here's how it works. Push the car or cars to be uncoupled until the couplers are above the magnet and stop. The magnet will start to pull the pins apart. Backing up slightly will separate the knuckles. Now, while the couplers are still pulled to the sides, ease back to the uncoupled car. The couplers will engage, but will be offset, so the knuckles won't couple. You can then keep pushing the car gently to its desired location. When you back away, the couplers will disengage and spring back to their normal positions.

Over the magnet, the couplers begin to separate when one car is backed up to create slack between the cars.

Pull one car away slightly and then move it back and the couplers will engage off-center and not lock.

Push the car to the desired location. When you pull one car away, the couplers will return to their normal position.

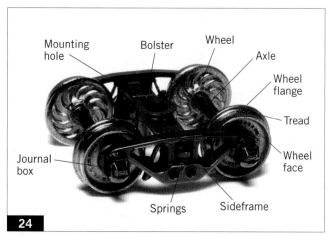

24

This is a Proto 2000 HO model of a 50-ton, solid-bearing, National B-1 freight-car truck. The model has a one-piece sideframe/bolster with metal wheels.

25

Micro-Trains offers several freight car trucks, including this solid-bearing design with coupler. The wheelsets are single-piece plastic moldings.

26

Roller-bearing trucks can be identified by the triangular end caps covering each axle end. This is an HO Walthers model of a modern center-beam flatcar.

27

Semi-scale HO wheels, including the Reboxx scale 33" ones at left, are narrower than standard RP-25 wheels such as the Kadee versions at right.

cars varies by railroad and era, but if you're concerned about such things, a good starting point is about half home road cars, about 25 percent cars from neighboring railroads, and the rest from railroads across the country.

The types of cars in the mix vary based on era. Boxcars were the most common car type into the 1960s; today, covered hoppers and tank cars hold that claim. Online industries also play a factor, If your small 1940s layout features a meat packing plant, you might have more refrigerator cars than boxcars.

Passenger car models

Unlike freight cars, passenger cars were often customized for specific railroads or trains. This can make it tough on modelers because many of these cars are appropriate for just one railroad and simply don't resemble cars from other railroads.

Fortunately, the last decade has seen an explosion in the number of well-detailed, ready-to-run passenger cars on the market in HO scale. From Fox Valley Models, Rapido, Walthers, and others, these cars feature interior detail, separately applied body and underbody details, and are patterned after cars in specific prototype passenger trains.

Full-length passenger car models range from 70 to 85 scale feet long. Running them on small layouts is a challenge, as they look awkward on tight curves, and a small train of just three or four cars plus a locomotive can overwhelm a layout. Keeping train lengths short and making curves as broad as possible are vital if you're interested in running passenger trains on a small layout.

Couplers

Once freight and passenger cars are on the layout and running, they shouldn't

require much (if any) maintenance. The area that requires the most care is couplers. Make sure initially that they're working properly, and they likely won't give you trouble in the future.

As mentioned in Chapter 10, through the 1990s, most rolling stock was equipped with horn-hook couplers (HO), **13**, or Rapido (N) couplers, **14**. These couplers were unrealistic and didn't operate well.

For years, Kadee (HO, S, and O) and Micro-Trains (N and Z) Magne-Matic automatic knuckle couplers were the aftermarket choice for serious modelers, **15**. They were about the only practical choice for couplers that looked realistic and operated well. The knuckles open and close to couple and uncouple, and the uncoupling pin (the curved steel pin under the coupler) allows the couplers to be uncoupled by an under-track magnet (see sidebar on page 85).

Freight car kits

Freight car kits range from simple and intermediate plastic models to craftsman-style, molded-resin kits. The keys to success are taking your time and being precise when cutting parts from sprues and gluing the parts together.

This Accurail HO stock car is an example of a simple kit. Assembling it was a matter of cutting a few parts from their sprues, pressing the doors into their brackets, and snapping the shell onto the frame. Note that the underbody brake detail is simple: a cylinder, control valve, and reservoir but no piping.

I attached the weight to the floor with double-sided foam tape—almost always a better choice than glue for this task.

I swapped the supplied couplers with Kadee no. 5 couplers as shown on page 83. The centering spring and coupler fit into the coupler box that's molded to the underframe, and the box cover presses in place with a friction pin. I also upgraded the wheelsets to a set of Reboxx 33"-diameter semi-scale wheels.

Beginning modelers are able to complete more-complex kits by going slow with each part and subassembly and making sure everything fits properly before moving to the next step.

Accurail's HO stock car is an easy-to-assemble plastic kit that builds into a nice model.

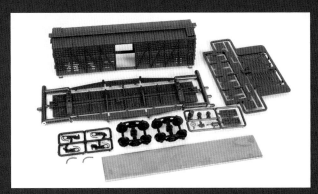

Here's what you get when you open the box.

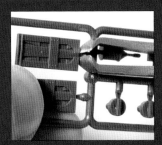

Use a sprue cutter to remove most parts from their sprues. The cutter leaves a clean separation with little or no cleanup required.

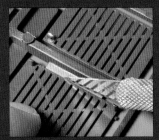

Cut the door from its sprue with a knife, carefully following the edge of the door for alignment. Make several light cuts instead of one heavy cut.

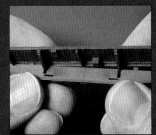

Fit the underbody parts into their mounting holes. Make sure parts are aligned before pressing them into place.

Glue underbody details in place by touching liquid plastic cement to each mounting peg with a brush.

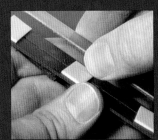

Secure the weight to the floor with a few short pieces of double-sided foam tape.

Dip a toothpick into cyanoacrylate adhesive (CA) and apply a drop to the door mounting pegs from the inside of the body.

Push the truck mounting pegs in place with needlenose pliers. Make sure the trucks can turn freely.

Tweezers help in positioning the brake staff and placing the brake wheel atop it. Drops of CA hold both in place.

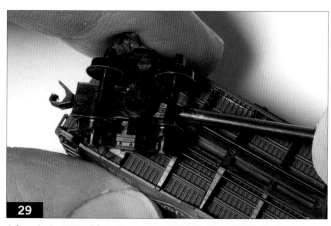

28 This N scale InterMountain solid-bearing truck is fitted with a pair of InterMountain scale 33"-diameter wheelsets.

29 A jeweler's screwdriver works for gently releasing the friction pins on N scale trucks. Don't damage details or the underframe when doing so.

As the patents on those couplers began to expire in the 1990s, several other manufacturers began offering compatible knuckle couplers, including Accurail (Accumate), Bachmann (EZ-Mate), McHenry, and Proto 2000 (Proto MAX). Almost all current ready-to-run rolling stock comes equipped with knuckle couplers.

Body-mounted couplers are now standard on most HO and larger equipment, but many N scale cars still have truck-mounted couplers. Body-mounted couplers are generally preferred for both realism and operation, although truck-mounted couplers allow running cars on tighter curves.

Couplers need to perform two tasks reliably: the shank needs to center itself when uncoupled, and the knuckle must remain closed unless the coupler is in the act of coupling or uncoupling. Springs of various types accomplish both.

Centering springs come in many designs. A bronze spring in a coupler pocket has long been the most common design for HO and larger scales, **16**. Other couplers use springs attached to each side of the coupler shank, **17**. Still others use coil or circular springs.

Most coupler knuckles in HO and larger scales are held in place with small coil springs. These will occasionally pop out during operation, so if a coupler suddenly starts misbehaving, this is the first area to check. To install a new spring (Kadee includes extra springs in most of its coupler kits), pick up the spring by gently sliding a hobby knife blade between coils near one end

of the spring. Fit the other end of the spring over one mounting peg and compress the spring until the near end slips over its mounting spring and pull the blade out, **18**.

Some couplers use thin plastic springs molded to the coupler to hold the knuckle in place, **19**. If these get forced into the open position for an extended period of time (in a storage box or in a line of cars on the layout), they can tend to take a set in that position and afterward fail to function properly. Avoid this style of coupler.

Other couplers—notably Accurail Accumate and Micro-Trains Magne-Matics—use a split-shank design with the knuckle on one half and the jaw on the other, **20**. The shank springs to open and close the knuckles as well.

Reliable couplers are critical to smooth operations. Couplers that are missing knuckle or centering springs, sag, are installed improperly, or are at the wrong height will cause problems such as derailments, difficult coupling, and unwanted uncoupling.

Kadee and Micro-Trains make coupler height gauges in most scales, **21**. It is important to get one and check every coupler on every car and locomotive. The top of the car's coupler should match the top of the coupler on the gauge, and the uncoupling pin (the curved metal wire under the coupler) should clear the bottom plate.

If a coupler is just a bit too low, it can be adjusted by adding a washer between the truck and the car kingpin, **22**. Kadee makes .010" and .015" washers in HO for this; in other

scales, you can make your own from sheet styrene plastic, but be careful not to raise the car height unrealistically.

If a coupler is a bit too tall, a shim (made from .010" to .020" sheet styrene) can often be added between the coupler box and the mounting area under the floor.

The best solution for either problem is to use a coupler with an overset or underset shank, **23**. Kadee and others make these in HO scale.

The coupler should center itself whenever it is moved. If it sticks off-center, open up the coupler box and check for anything that might be binding it: stray plastic flash on the box, a metal burr or plastic flash on the coupler shank, or a broken whisker spring.

Replacing couplers on most modern equipment is a matter of opening the coupler box, taking out the original coupler and spring, and substituting a new coupler in its place.

Some modelers prefer to cut off or remove uncoupling pins for better appearance (adding more-realistic air hose details to cars instead), but doing this eliminates the ability to magnetically uncouple cars.

You can also uncouple cars with a hand tool. The Accurail Switchman is one commercial version; a fine screwdriver or stick with a wedge-shaped end will also work. Slip the tool between the knuckles and give the tool a gentle twist.

Wheels and trucks

Freight and passenger cars have a truck at each end. The truck is the assembly

30

Turning Micro-Mark's Truck Tuner in an HO plastic truck frame will clean the bearing surfaces.

31

A National Model Railroad Association standards gauge is handy for making sure that wheelsets are in gauge.

that holds the wheelsets; a wheelset is two wheels mounted on an axle, **24**. Most trucks have two axles and four wheels; many early heavyweight passenger cars rode on six-wheel trucks, and some heavy-duty freight cars also ride on six-wheel trucks. Many N scale trucks include couplers, **25**.

Prototype trucks have been built to many designs. The car kingpin sits on the center of the truck bolster, which runs from sideframe to sideframe. The ends of the bolster sit on springs within the sideframes to help cushion and smooth the ride.

Through the 1950s, solid-bearing trucks were standard. These had a journal box covering each wheel bearing, with a lid that opened to reveal a pack of balled-up cotton (called waste). Opening the lid allowed these to be oiled, which needed to be done frequently. If a bearing ran dry it would quickly overheat and catch fire, which could burn through the journal.

By the 1960s, cars with roller-bearing trucks became common, **26**. The roller bearings offered much less resistance and they were sealed, removing the need for repeated lubrication. The bearing end caps on these trucks have a distinctive look as they turn as the car rolls along.

Most model trucks have frames molded in engineering plastic, although some (Kadee and others) offer cast-metal versions. Wheelsets can be a single injection-molded piece or plastic wheels on a metal axle, but most higher-quality cars have metal wheels mounted on a plastic or a nonmagnetic

metal axle, so they are not attracted by under-track uncoupling magnets.

Experienced modelers prefer metal wheels for several reasons. They are heavier than plastic wheels and lower the car's center of gravity. Metal wheels tend to polish themselves on the rails while moving, keeping themselves and the rails clean, whereas plastic wheels tend to accumulate dirt and grime. With a more realistic profile and shape, metal wheels also look better.

Replacement wheelsets are available with varying wheel diameters, wheel widths, and axle widths, **27** and **28**. If you're swapping out wheelsets (upgrading from plastic to metal, for example), make sure replacements are the proper size. Older freight cars and modern 70-ton capacity cars ride on 33"-diameter wheels; the 100-ton capacity cars common today ride on 36"-diameter wheels.

In HO, many replacement wheels are labeled as semi-scale, meaning they're narrower than the NMRA standard (RP25) wheel, which is quite a bit wider than a real wheel but not as narrow as real wheels (which wouldn't operate well over scale turnouts). Semi-scale wheels are a nice compromise between the two.

You can replace wheelsets simply by spreading the sideframe slightly with your fingers, taking the old ones out, and slipping the new ones in. You can also replace the entire truck with a better or more highly detailed version.

Most trucks in HO and larger scales are held by screws; many N scale and some HO models use friction pins.

Remove these by gently pulling on the trucks. If that doesn't work, use a thin screwdriver to gently pry the truck loose, **29**. Don't gouge the underframe when doing this.

Wheelsets should spin freely in their trucks. If they bind, remove the wheelsets and look for stray material in the pockets where the wheelsets rest. Micro-Mark offers a sideframe reaming tool (the Truck Tuner) in HO scale that cleans and enlarges the pocket, **30**. Do not oil sideframes or axle ends. This will only cause dirt to accumulate and hamper operations.

Make sure wheelsets are in gauge, **31**. (The NMRA offers standards gauges in all scales—pick one up for your scale.) Wheelsets that are wide or narrow in gauge can easily derail. You can usually correct the gauge by grabbing one wheel firmly in each hand and twisting while pulling the axle in or out.

Cars should roll smoothly down the tracks. If a car wobbles excessively, you can fix it by adjusting the trucks. Start by tightening one of the truck mounting screws until the truck begins to bind and then loosen it a quarter-turn—just enough for it to swivel freely. Do the same to the other truck, but loosen it more—about a half turn. This should restrict the wobbling, but still allow enough play for the trucks to flex over turnouts and uneven track. It's a bit tougher to do this if a car's trucks are held by pins instead of screws, but try to do the same, tightening one pin so that the truck has just enough room to swivel.

1

CHAPTER TWELVE

Painting and weathering

A great way to weather freight cars is to give them a dusting of chalk that is close to the color of the car. This will fade the lettering and flatten the overall finish, giving it a weatherbeaten, oxidized appearance.

In the "old days" of the hobby, a lot of painting was required to get models ready for a layout. Often the only way to get the locomotives and rolling stock you wanted was to paint and decal them yourself. Today a tremendous range of paint schemes are available that are more detailed and accurate than were models of the past. You'll still find it handy to paint details and apply chalk weathering to get your equipment and structures ready for the layout, 1.

2

Model paints include, from left, Model Master enamel and Acryl (acrylic) lines, Badger Modelflex (acrylic), acrylic craft paints such as Delta Ceramcoat, and Polly Scale (acrylic).

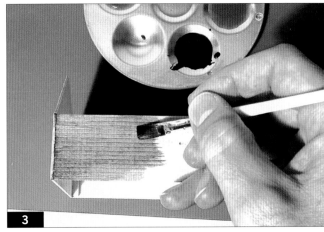

3

Wood can be stained by thin mixes of acrylic paints. Dip the brush in paint, then in water, and then brush the wood. Small metal palettes are inexpensive and handy for holding small amounts of paint.

4

You'll find a variety of brushes handy. Here's a ¾" flat sable, ¼" synthetic, no. 3 sable, no. 0 camel hair, no. 0 synthetic, and 3/0 sable.

5

Flat brushes work well for painting smooth surfaces. Here, I'm brush-painting Polly Scale Concrete on the base of the structure from Chapter 8.

Types of paint

Model paints include acrylics (water-based), enamels, and lacquers. All will do a good job of painting models, and all will work well on most materials including plastic, brass, resin, and wood, **2**.

I highly recommend water-based paints for modeling. The fumes from lacquers and enamels (and their thinners) are hazardous to breathe, and wearing a facemask cartridge respirator is cumbersome. They should only be used with adequate ventilation.

The quality of today's acrylic paints, such as Badger ModelFlex and Floquil Polly Scale, is very good—much improved over acrylic paints of the 1970s and '80s. Cleanup is also easy. Here are a few tips to keep in mind with acrylics.

Mix the paint well before using. Depending upon how long the bottle has been sitting, you may have to stir it with a toothpick or a small stirring stick to get all of the pigment mixed. You can shake the bottle as well, but if you do this, let the paint sit for a bit so any air bubbles disappear before painting.

Air is the main enemy of acrylic paint. Keep paint bottles closed as much as possible to keep air away from the paint. Transferring paint as needed to a palette or tray as needed will avoid open bottles, **3**.

Paint that dries on lids and the lip and threads of the bottle can contaminate the paint—once acrylic paint dries, it will remain a solid. Before you put a lid back onto a paint bottle, wipe the threads clean on both the cap and bottle and wipe all paint from the rim of the bottle as well. If you open a bottle and find a skin has formed over the paint, be sure to remove it completely with a toothpick.

Paint brushes

You'll need a selection of brushes for various types of work, **4**. You don't need to spend a fortune on them, but you'll want brushes a step up from the 10-for-a-dollar variety. Synthetic and sable work well when you need a smooth finish; camel hair is less expensive and good for general-purpose touch-up work. Flat brushes are measured by their width. Round brushes are numbered: the larger the number, the larger the brush.

6

Shiny wheels aren't realistic. Painting them grimy black and dark rust colors improves their appearance.

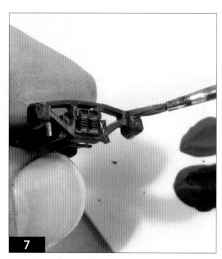

7

Get rid of the plastic appearance of truck sideframes by painting them. I mix brown and black on the brush for a varied look.

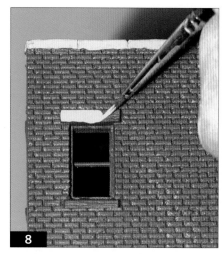

8

Look for door and window trim as well as other details on structures that can be painted.

9

Wood structures can easily be brush-painted. Follow the siding pattern and brush the wet paint back into the previously painted areas.

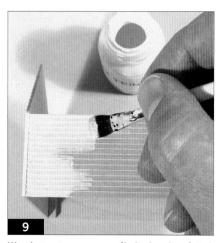

11

Scalecoat, Floquil, Model Master, and Testors all offer a variety of railroad colors and clear coats in spray cans. Krylon and other non-model paints can also be used.

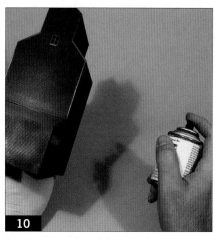

10

Spray cans work well for painting structures and freight cars. A latex glove will keep paint off of your hand.

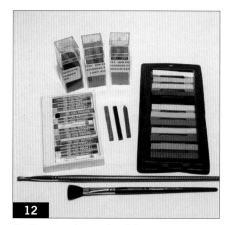

12

Chalk comes in powdered form, or you can make your own by scraping artist's pastel chalks. You can apply chalks with a stiff brush, such as a hog bristle (top) or a soft synthetic brush, depending upon the effect you're simulating.

Good-quality brushes will last a long time if you take care of them properly. For starters, when painting, keep the paint on the ends of the bristles, not up to the ferrule (the metal part that holds the bristles in place). If dried paint gets into the ferrule, the bristles will splay out, making it tough to control the brush.

Wet the brush with water (for acrylics) or paint thinner (for lacquers or enamels) before using it. This will help keep paint from drying quickly on the bristles and make cleanup much easier.

Clean each brush thoroughly after every use. Do not simply let brushes soak in water or thinner. To clean a brush after using water-base paints, rinse it under running water. Work a bit of dish detergent into the bristles, then rinse it thoroughly until no trace of paint is left. Dry the brush with a towel or paper towel, pulling gently outward on the bristles so that the brush retains its shape. For enamels or lacquers, swish the brush in thinner. Pull the brush through a paper towel to remove paint and repeat the process until no paint is visible. Store brushes bristle-end up in a plastic cup or other container.

Painting techniques

To paint a large surface, use a flat synthetic or sable brush, 5. Start at one edge and keep brush strokes in one direction. Don't overbrush—let the

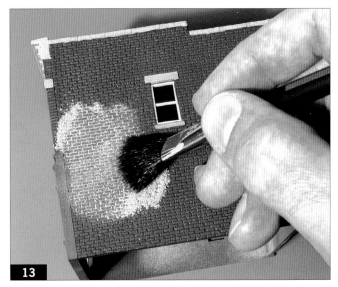

13

Simulate brick mortar by brushing gray chalk onto the wall surface. The chalk will tend to stick in the recesses. You can wipe the brick surface if you wish or leave it for an oxidized appearance. A light coat of flat finish will seal the chalk.

paint settle on its own. If you go over the paint more than two times, brush strokes will remain in the surface. Get more paint on the brush and apply it just away from the previously applied paint, using a brush stroke to bring it back and slightly overlap it.

You can stain wood with a paint wash as in photo **3**. Alternate dipping your brush in paint and water and then streak it on the wood for various effects. Black, gray, boxcar red, mineral red, rail brown, and other colors will produce different effects.

Look for details to paint to increase realism. Give wheel faces a coat of dark rust-colored paint, **6**, and paint truck sideframes grimy black and rust, **7**. Many structures have trim that needs to be painted, **8**.

Wood structures need painting. I like to prime them with latex flat interior primer, **9**, followed by a finish color if needed. Prime both sides of each wall to prevent warping. If you have a gallon can, you can use an eyedropper to transfer some paint into a two-ounce jar to keep it handy for modeling projects.

Plastic structures are often molded in realistic colors, but plastic tends to have a shiny appearance. You can brush-paint plastic structures or paint them with a spray can, **10**, which is especially handy for large buildings. A coat of clear flat finish, such as Model Master flat or Testor's Dullcote,

will also help eliminate the plastic appearance.

Floquil, Scalecoat, and Testors all offer spray paint, **11**. There are many store brands as well but be aware that these sometimes have pigment that is not as fine as model paints.

Only use spray cans in a vented spray booth or outdoors. Make sure the can is warm—placing it in a warm tray of water for five minutes will help. Shake it thoroughly. Spray in quick bursts, passing quickly from side to side over the model. Overlap each pass slightly. Make sure each coat dries before adding another.

Airbrushing is a handy technique to know, and it's the best way to get a smooth finish on a locomotive shell or freight car. Airbrushing techniques go beyond the scope of this book, but if you're interested, take a look at the book *Basic Painting and Weathering for Model Railroaders* (Kalmbach Books, 2003).

Chalks

Chalks are another handy, quick way to weather and finish models, **12**. You can buy powdered weathering colors from AIM and Bar Mills, or you can make your own by scraping artist's pastel chalks with a hobby knife. For good results, use artist-quality chalks, which have better pigment than kids' playground chalk.

The key to success with working with chalks is applying them to a flat-finish

14

Black chalk does a nice job of simulating exhaust grime and stains on the stacks and roofs of diesel locomotives.

surface. Chalk simply won't stick well to semigloss or gloss surfaces so give such structures or rolling stock a light coat of clear flat before applying chalks.

You can simulate brick mortar with chalk by applying it to a structure side and working it in with a brush, **13**. Seal the chalk with a light coat of clear finish. If you keep the sealing coat light, and you've applied the chalk to a flat finish, most of the effect should remain.

Chalks are also great for weathering freight cars and locomotives, **1** and **14**. Use black for simulating exhaust and soot stains and black and dark gray for grime. You can match the car color to create the effect of faded lettering and choose various browns and dark reds for capturing rust.

Manufacturers and suppliers

Accurail (rolling stock and details)
www.accurail.com

AIM Products (scenery)
www.aimprodx.com

Alkem Scale Models (structures, details)
alkemscalemodels.net

Amaco (Sculptamold)
www.amaco.com

American Model Builders (structures, details)
www.laserkit.com

American Models (S scale products)
www.americanmodels.com

Arizona Rock & Mineral (scenery)
www.rrscenery.com

Athearn (model railroad products)
www.athearn.com

Atlas Model Railroad Co. and Atlas O
(model railroad products)
www.atlasrr.com

Bachmann (model railroad products)
www.bachmanntrains.com

Badger Air Brush Co. (paint)
www.badger-airbrush.com

Bar Mills (structures, details)
www.barmillsmodels.com

Blair Line (signs, structures)
www.blairline.com

Bluford Shops (rolling stock)
www.bluford-shops.com

Bowser (locomotives, rolling stock)
www.bowser-trains.com

Branchline (rolling stock)
www.branchline-trains.com

Caboose Industries (turnout controls)
www.cabooseind.com

Circuitron (switch machines, electronics)
www.circuitron.com

City Classics (structures, details)
www.cityclassics.biz

Classic Metal Works (vehicles)
www.classicmetalworks.com

Clover House
(dry transfers, details, scratchbuilding materials)
www.cloverhouse.com

Con-Cor (model railroad products)
www.con-cor.com

CVP Products (DCC supplies)
www.cvpusa.com

DeLuxe Innovations (rolling stock)
www.deluxeinnovations.com

Design Preservation Models (structures)
See Woodland Scenics

Digitrax (DCC supplies)
www.digitrax.com

Eastern Seaboard Models Corporation
(freight cars)
www.esmc.com

ExactRail (rolling stock)
www.exactrail.com

Floquil (paint)
see Testor Corp.

Fox Valley Models (model railroad products)
www.foxvalleymodels.com

Hot Wire Foam Factory (foam cutting tools)
www.hotwirefoamfactory.com

InterMountain Railway
(model railroad supplies)
www.intermountain-railway.com

JL Innovative Design (structures and details)
www.jlinnovative.com

Kadee (rolling stock and couplers)
www.kadee.com

Kato (model railroad products)
www.katousa.com

Lenz (DCC supplies)
www.lenz.com

Life-Like (model railroad products)
See Wm. K. Walthers

McHenry (couplers)
www.mchenrycouplers.com

Microscale (decals)
www.microscale.com

Micro-Mark (tools and supplies)
www.micromark.com

Micro-Trains Line (model railroad supplies)
www.micro-trains.com

Midwest Products
(cork roadbed and materials)
www.midwestproducts.com

Model Rectifier Corp. (electronics and control)
www.modelrec.com

NJ International (electronics and control)
www.njinternational.com

Noch (scenery products)
See Wm. K. Walthers

North Coast Engineering (DCC supplies)
www.ncedcc.com

Peco (track)
See Wm. K. Walthers

Pikestuff (structures)
See Rix Products

Proto 2000 (model railroad products)
See Wm. K. Walthers

Proto Power West/A-Line
(rolling stock, details)
www.ppw-aline.com

Rapido Trains (model railroad products)
www.rapidotrains.com

Red Caboose (rolling stock)
www.red-caboose.com

Rix Products (model railroad products)
www.rixproducts.com

S-Helper Service (S scale trains)
www.showcaseline.com

Scenic Express (scenery products)
www.scenicexpress.com

Soundtraxx (DCC decoders)
www.soundtraxx.com

Testor Corp. (paint)
www.testors.com

Tomalco (S scale track)
www.tomalcotrack.com

Trainworx (rolling stock)
www.train-worx.com

Trix (track)
See Wm. K. Walthers

Wm. K. Walthers
(model railroad products)
www.walthers.com

Woodland Scenics
(scenery, structures and details)
www.woodlandscenics.com

Xuron (tools)
www.xuron.com

About the author

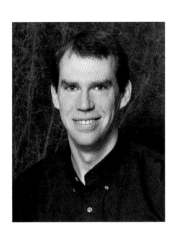

Jeff Wilson has written more than 20 books on railroads and model rail-roading. He spent 10 years as an associate editor at *Model Railroader* magazine, and he currently works as a freelance writer, editor, and photographer, contributing articles to MR and other magazines. He enjoys many facets of the hobby, especially building structures and detailing locomotives, as well as photographing both real and model railroads. Jeff enjoys baseball, and during summer, he occasionally operates the scoreboard at Miller Park for the Milwaukee Brewers.

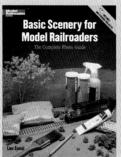  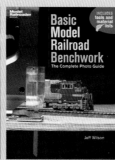 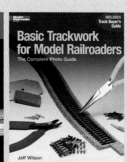 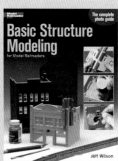 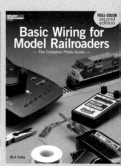